Sabina Jeschke, Frank Hees,
Anja Richert, Sven Trantow (Eds.)

Prethinking Work

Arbeitswissenschaften

Band 7

LIT

PRETHINKING WORK

Insights on the Future of Work

edited by

Sabina Jeschke, Frank Hees,
Anja Richert, Sven Trantow

LIT

The project on which this publication is based received funding from the Federal Ministry of Education and Research (ALK00200) and the European Social Fund.
Responsibility for the contents of the publication lies with the authors.

SPONSORED BY THE

Federal Ministry of Education and Research

ESF Europäischer Sozialfonds für Deutschland

The book has been printed with friendly assistance of the RWTH Aachen University.

RWTH AACHEN UNIVERSITY

This book is printed on acid-free paper.

Bibliographic information published by the Deutsche Nationalbibliothek
The Deutsche Nationalbibliothek lists this publication in the Deutsche Nationalbibliografie; detailed bibliographic data are available in the Internet at http://dnb.d-nb.de.

ISBN 978-3-643-90240-5

A catalogue record for this book is available from the British Library

Klosbachstr. 107
CH-8032 Zürich
Tel. +41 (0) 44-251 75 05
Fax +41 (0) 44-251 75 06
e-Mail: zuerich@lit-verlag.ch
http://www.lit-verlag.ch

LIT VERLAG Dr. W. Hopf
Berlin 2012
Fresnostr. 2
D-48159 Münster
Tel. +49 (0) 2 51-620 320
Fax +49 (0) 2 51-23 19 72
e-Mail: lit@lit-verlag.de
http://www.lit-verlag.de

Distribution:
In Germany: LIT Verlag Fresnostr. 2, D-48159 Münster
Tel. +49 (0) 2 51-620 32 22, Fax +49 (0) 2 51-922 60 99, e-mail: vertrieb@lit-verlag.de

In Austria: Medienlogistik Pichler-ÖBZ, e-mail: mlo@medien-logistik.at

In Switzerland: B + M Buch- und Medienvertrieb, e-mail: order@buch-medien.ch

In the UK: Global Book Marketing, e-mail: mo@centralbooks.com

Contents

Workplace Innovation

Introduction

Sven Trantow, Anja Richert, Frank Hees and Sabina Jeschke

Work is a systematically relevant element of the global economy. It generates value, it allows innovation and it is a fundamental prerequisite for all conceivable economic activity. Moreover, work is a central part of our everyday life and a reflection of our societal conditions and developments. Globalization, virtualization, automation, acceleration and flexibilization represent only a few of the strong drivers that determine work in the 21st century. "Prethinking Work" asks for the most important trends, opportunities and risks in the future working environment.

The "International Monitoring" (IMO)[1] research and development project brought together researcher, economic actors and politicians from twelve different countries to come up with answers to the question about the future of work and therewith about the future of our social and economic reality. Since these topics are generally of enormous significance to everyone, "Prethinking Work" is addressed to a broad audience, aiming at representing the knowledge of international experts in comprehensible and illustrative terms beyond traditional expert jargon.

That is the reason for an extraordinary book design: Using only the – very limited! – space of two pages, the authors describe what they believe to be the most important developments and challenges of the modern working world and, based on these, provide recommendations for how to design work in the early 21st century. For many of our authors, the format of a brief and succinct prognosis was a new and challenging exercise. However, it has been worth it: Their efforts have resulted in an unusual, trans-disciplinary and inspiring anthology that provides diverse and entertaining insights into different aspects of the future world of work based on the broad experiences of our international experts.

The contributions can, despite the breadth of topics covered in this anthology, clearly be divided into six different sections with a specific focus each:

Working Society

As the world of work changes completely, so do the meaning work has for humans, and the relationship between work and society. It is becoming more and more difficult to distinguish and separate work from leisure and our personal lives. At the same time, work pressure and workload keep increasing within the crippled capitalist world economy. It may sound like a paradox, but it seems that humans both need work and, at the same time, have too much of it.

In his contribution, *Werner Wobbe* describes what the critical social parameters and challenges of work look like in 21st century Europe. *Milena Jostmeier* reflects on the fundamental

[1] The IMO project is implemented by the institute cluster IMA/ZLW & IfU – Institute of Information Management in Mechanical Engineering (IMA), Center for Learning and Knowledge Management (ZLW) and Assoc. Institute for Management Cybernetics (IfU) of the RWTH Aachen University – and funded by the German Federal Ministry of Education and Research, and the European Social Fund.

individual, social and economic use of work. But does that mean that we all have to work that much? *Heather Hofmeister* drills deeper: Do we have to allow work to dominate our lives? Do we live in order to work, or do we work in order to live? *Stella Fleischer* provides insights on the role of neoliberal economic ideologies play in answering these questions. And while *Barbara Light* has ideas for modifying capitalist working conditions, she cannot see any need to regress to the past.

Human Workforce

Demographic changes, a lack of skilled personnel, as well as the increasing role that knowledge and skills will play in creating economic value have turned human labor into one of the fundamental assets of companies. In this context, the term human capital reflects both the increasing economic significance of humans, as well as their ruthless economization.

Thomas Wallner describes the special position of humans in advanced industrial societies and advocates for overcoming Tayloristic organization of work. Against the backdrop of increased flexibilization of work and the reduction of core staffs to cloud working, *Charlie Grantham* forecasts the return of guilds, which workers can use to organize and market themselves. Using the Chilean labor market as an example, *Patrizio Tonelli* shows how a lack of common representation and collective bargaining results in precarious working conditions. The health risks and economic damage caused by future working conditions are identified in intentionally dystopian statements by *Lena Hünefeld* and *Larissa Müller*, while *Frank Striewe* and *Markus Schwering* take a closer look at the myth of participation as a strain buffer.

Collective Competence

In the context of highly dynamic work demands and a knowledge half-life that continues to decrease, purely professional qualifications will not be sufficient to ensure the employability of individuals over their continuously expanding working life. Companies need people who can work on teams and can communicate, who can learn independently and adjust their skills continuously to new demands. Here, both individualized learning as well as the organization's use of competences will increasingly align themselves with the principles of collectivity and networking.

Leif Edvinsson sketches out the potential of human networking and collective learning processes for meeting social challenges. At the level of organizations, *Christina Öberg* shows the advantages and disadvantages of project-based competence nets. Against the background of demographic changes, *Gabriele Hoeborn* and *Jennifer Bredtmann* describe the necessity of forming innovative professional communities, as well as age-specific and individualized options for learning. *Yvonne Salazar* explains the requirements skills development in companies will have to meet in future, and how the boundaries between work and learning continue to blur. And finally, *Kayano Fukuda* describes the integration of consumers' external competences for co-creating new functionalities beyond purely economic value.

Innovation Culture

In future, innovation will continue to be a leading paradigm of economic action in advanced industrial societies – companies will need to produce innovations on an ongoing basis in order to ensure their competitiveness in dynamic world markets. Innovation-oriented corporate culture will be a critical fertile ground for innovative activity at all levels of an organization. Here, the standard practices of companies in the future will include opening up innovation processes and integrating external stakeholders.

To what extent Open Innovation can be expanded into a comprehensive concept of Open Working is demonstrated by *Keith Bevis* und *Mariana Dodourova*, while *Birgit Fingerle*, *Anna Maria Köck* and *Klaus Tochtermann* shine a light on the individual and organizational challenges of this new openness. *Peter Brödner* underlines the fundamental importance of human working capacity and its adequate handling for innovation and future knowledge work. *Celina Proch* and *Agata Siuda* focus on the linkage between companies and creatives, while *Martin Kamprath* highlights the creation of symbolic value for successful innovations in the form of corporate celebrities. Since innovation processes always involve uncertainty and unpredictability, *Kirsimarja Blomqvist's* contribution points out the increasing significance of organizational trust in the work world of the future.

Virtual Work

Automation, digitization, and virtualization of the working world will continue to proceed. Not only because of the technological trends, but also particularly, because of the increasing pressure to make things more flexible: work must be doable everywhere and all the time. In order to implement such all-encompassing mobility, information will be moved instead of the people. Human communication processes are moving from physical to virtual reality – thanks to a networked and digitized world.

What will be possible in future and beyond today's social media tools is described by *Eilif Trondsen* using a fictitious job in 2020. Here, the technical barriers for virtual work and life in the cloud have, according to *Uwe Hauck*, already been conquered, and as *Marc Paczian* points out, the socio-cultural conditions exist too: humans are ready for a virtual world of work – while some of the companies are still caught up in the traditional paradigm. But things are in motion here too. *Lauge Baungaard Rasmussen* describes the essential factors for successful design of virtual teamwork while *Sebastiaan Meijer* writes about experiences with using serious games in participatory change processes. In his vision of a society that is totally networked mentally, *Stephen Downes* forecasts the paths a comprehensive virtualization of work and life will take in future.

Workplace Innovation

For a long time, innovation was regarded from a very product- and technology-centered perspective. Given the increasing significance of humans for the innovative capability and for the competitiveness of organizations, the focus is expanded by the dimensions of social and organizational innovations. Changes in human behavior patterns and organizational parameters hold enormous promise of innovation and will, in future, be on an equal footing with product and technological developments – including the economic aspect.

Jürgen Howaldt, *Ralf Kopp* and *Frank Pot* outline a holistic approach for Workplace Innovation that will increase both organizational performance as well as the quality of work through social, organizational and technological innovations. What an innovation-oriented and people-centered work environment can look like is described by *Thomas Fundneider* and *Markus Peschl*, while *Sven Schimpf* and *Flavius Sturm* discuss the key trends in future work design in the R&D area. *Frank Emspak* compares two diametrically opposed but nevertheless successful formats of work organization using the examples of Chinese company Foxconn and the transparent Volkswagen factory in Germany. Finally, despite all the dynamics and future changes forecast, *Hans-Georg Schnauffer* stops for a moment and points out four characteristics of knowledge-intensive work places which – despite all prophecies of doom – are not going to change in the future, after all.

The 32 articles from authors of twelve different countries outline decisive developments and challenges of the future world of work. The contributions make obvious that work is primarily changing its form whereas its meaning and relevance will remain unchanged: Work was, is and will be an essential element of successful socioeconomic systems. Its systemic relevance implies an important obligation for politicians, economic actors and researchers. It implies the obligation to actively design the future of work in order to meet the economic and societal needs of work in the future.

Working Society

European Grand Societal Challenges for Work in the 21st Century

Werner Wobbe

The concept of the German and Scandinavian welfare states was based on large public and private enterprises with high trade union power and co-determination which had their heyday in the 1970s. Thoughts and reasoning in the 21st century about work design often have that specific working environment in mind. However, the situation has changed dramatically. The preconditions of the welfare state of the past were the following: the social and economic system competition of the East/West conflict; countries were able to regulate their internal distributive conflicts; large public enterprises were a welfare state by themselves (postal services, railways, communal or regional utilities); large private corporations had production and the main market at home like the automobile manufacturing, chemical and pharmaceutical industries as well as steel companies; large private enterprises again were comprehensive entities of the manufacturing value chain integrating all the services the company needed.

The big national conglomerates were the blueprint for good industrial work. The glamour of their working conditions gave rise to biased favorable opinions on future work developments. Nevertheless, these biased views overlooked the fact that the majority of jobs in SMEs had much poorer working conditions.

What Destroyed the Golden Prospects?

The model of a regulated, "cozy", and hardly competitive work environment was not only challenged by the globalization but also by accounting practices introduced by multinational companies. The fall of the Berlin Wall ended a type of system competition aiming at highest social welfare and launched the current system of competition based on global financial governance. Big national enterprises quickly expanded into multinationals and, in doing so, became independent of the nation-state. In front of these developments were U.S. corporations pioneering a financial management of companies. Instrumental to those management practices were global investment opportunities and information technology. Outsourcing, concentration on core-business, expanding into new markets and production sites using internal corporate trading and tax management have blown away any hope of further expanding the golden age of "cozy" working conditions. Increased global competition – even within the company– is a factor that is shaping the modern work environment.

Good Work Will Be Shaped by Economic Specialization

The current discussion about the euro crisis has shed light on competitive economic structures of the European Union and its Member States, its economic capabilities and specificities shaping the conditions for work. Hence, a region's industrial/economic structure determines the kind of work it offers its citizens. An increasing industrial specialization and division of work in Europe has emerged. Germany and Sweden, for instance, have a strong electromechanical sector with automobiles and machines while France is strong in food and luxury products, the United Kingdom specializes in financial services and many Mediterranean regions are strong in tourism. The internal European market has fostered the notion of specialization and will continue to do so in an effort to safeguard or even achieve higher value-added production or services. The winners of that development will be able to achieve higher value creation through "smart specialization" if they build the right supporting infrastructures for specialization.

And What Are the Prospects for Work?

Industrial work will not disappear. It will, however, become more knowledge-intensive and particularly specialized in Europe's leading economic regions. To stay at the cutting edge, economic activities have to choose their areas of specialization wisely and avoid direct competition in areas where others outperform. The activities have to follow the accelerated pace for new services, products and innovation.

The "Grand Societal Challenges" are an anticipation of prospective European social and economic developments. These challenges also allow foreseeing new demand, new markets, new economic sectors and new work. Grand Challenges are associated with demographic changes such as ageing and health, the bio-economy and food security, sustainable energy, green transport, resource efficiency, raw materials and safe societies. The future of work related to the Grand Challenges may be characterized as follows: new jobs in ageing and health will open up in the pharmaceutical industry including biotech/ pharmaceuticals, medicine especially in high-tech medicine and in medical devices. These sectors will provide high paying jobs. The healthcare and wellbeing sector may offer the bulk of jobs. However, the jobs available may only fall into the low to middle income range. Food security will become a science-based sector and will have a strong arm in biotechnology. The bio-economy may offer the bulk of jobs in agriculture with average incomes. Sustainable energy which foresees decentralized energy production, energy savings and efficiency gains will favor traditional electro-technical jobs and can sustain their survival in Europe. Green transport aims at innovation in the traditional transport industries and may stabilize jobs in these industries. Resource efficiency and raw materials foster high-value jobs in science and the chemical industry. Safe societies will account for the bulk of low-paid security jobs from concierge services to private corporate security and to military and defense. The latter may be organized at the European level. Mid-value social and educational work is in high demand and will expand as well as those jobs in defense which are related to high-tech solutions protecting the ageing western population against the upheaval in the poorer and overpopulated rest of the world.

The highest risk for work in Europe in the context of a global free trade area is having no work or keeping work of low value. The way forward is innovation towards high quality products and services to boost the welfare. Forward looking regions would enter into smart specialization and respond to new societal challenges by offering specific products and services.

Reflecting on Work as a Societal Need

Milena Jostmeier

Work is a critical determinant of human life.It is a necessary prerequisite for the reproduction of human life organized in societies, thus fundamentally determining the quality of the individual and the collective access to lifeworld in toto. Given this, the societal need to keep continuously an abstracting and differentiating eye on the *quality* of work, cannot be overestimated in its importance. Work is not only a means for satisfying (and creating) economic and societal needs, but it can also be seen as an important way for individuals to find fulfillment. The individual and social desire for self-determination finds its central expression influencing the design, and thus the quality of work. This makes work a political issue. The (labor policy) goal of designing work to be human-oriented competes – not necessarily incompatibly – with the goal of increasing efficiency and maximizing profits. During times of growing global competitive pressure, this is a particularly difficult task. But arguments for why society's discussion about the quality of work must not suffer the fate of a "would-like-to-have"-debate do not 'only' result from the significance work has for each individual, but also from the significance the quality of work has for society.

Work is relevant for individuals:

People spend a majority of their (life-)time working. The working conditions individuals face, the quality of their work, impact their subjective physical, mental and emotional resources such as their health or creativity. What type of paid work people do has a major impact on their social position. Individuals who do not have a paid job are often relegated to the margins of society. Their usefulness for the social collective is being questioned.

Work is relevant for society:

It is not only the distribution of work that has an impact on a society's social structure – represented e.g.by the correlation between education/training and income or lifestyle. The quality of work significantly contributes to the extent to which an individual can contribute to society, and whether s/he can use and advance her/his potential. Working conditions that make people sick, resulting in mental/emotional exhaustion, e.g., cause very high costs at the macroeconomic level due to high levels of absence from work or disability.

Work is relevant for companies:

In addition, it becomes apparent at the organizational level that work that is conducive to health and creativity is used for increasing an organization's ability to innovate. New organizational innovation strategies increasingly focus on subjective resources in the form of an opening-up of the innovation process, such as by integrating consumers, or using non-linear organizational formats with reflexive or participatory structural elements. It is the individual (within a team) that responds to unexpected events or is able to develop new things creatively. His/her motivation and ability to act are essential variables in fostering innovation.

Integrating Work and Innovation Research in Germany

The funding program "Working – Learning – Developing skills. Potential for Innovation in a Modern Working Environment" of the German Ministry of Education and Research examines design approaches that have a synergy effect in this regard: having both, a focus on promoting individuals' personalities as well as on fostering companies' and networks' ability to innovate. It represents an understanding of innovation that is no longer looking only at technological innovations. In an economy dominated by new (hybrid) production and service formats, depending on constantly renewing knowledge, innovation policy has to consider the promotion of social and (inter-)organizational innovations as an equivalent goal. Against this background, and including technology development, work research can analyze and foster social innovations, thus representing an essential dimension that cuts across innovation research and promotion.

Germany has a longer tradition, with changing approaches and scopes, in doing application oriented research and design of work in a (democratic) dialog with actors from academe, business, politics and different interest groups. Here, the variety of the different research and development types must be systematically evaluated, advanced along and aligned with the changing and, in some instances, diverging needs of academe, companies and employees. Transdisciplinary, applicationoriented formats require valid structural analyses that will provide the definition of the existing empirical status quo. Consequently, transdisciplinary research must not drift off into mere design and consulting activities focusing on individual cases. Politicians and scientists are challenged to warrant the scientific acquisition of fundamental knowledge in this area and – also with regard to promoting innovation – apply it systematically.

The significance of work for the different levels of society results in a need for a broad societal discourse about the quality of work.This need will continue to become more obvious as the growing global competition and the rapidly increasing dependence of the economy on knowledge makes work a critical factor for innovation. Public funding for work research can be seen politically as a long-term investment into the economic as well as cultural ability to innovate, but also into social cohesion and equity. Good work – or at least, work that preserve people's health- should, however, not 'only' be a *means* to the end of an economic innovation capability; it should be a *goal* that is shared by society.

The King, Cinderella, and 168 Hours: Work and *Free Space* in Historical and Life Course Perspective

Heather Hofmeister

I'm writing this at my home office on a snowy February morning. The topic *Prethinking work* invites me to reflect on the prefix *pre*, sending my thoughts to previous historical times. And since this reflection should be about pre*thinking* work, then I'll go with my gut – what do I *feel* about work? Finally, what is *work*? Here we go, using the work of writing to illustrate.

Revolutions in Writing a Text

If it were 1700, as a professional writer I'd be a man, writing with an ink pen on paper at home. I would have the luxury to concentrate because servants would be taking care of the household and children. If it were 1900, a professional writer would still be a man, writing by hand, in an office. If it were 1950, my female secretary or I might type the manuscript, in an office. Here in 2012, I'm a woman (revolutionary) working at home again (revolutionary), but without servants (revolutionary); instead, a highly differentiated labor market and my own time management plus advanced technologies make household management somehow possible (revolutionary). Technology, for example, makes it possible for me to write, edit, and send this piece instantly from home.

Human Beings, not Human Doings

How privileged this working situation is! I'm at home putting thoughts into a beautifully formatted document, cup of tea at my side, dog under the desk, as snow falls outside. On the other hand, the work has no end. No one limits my work hours. New requests, demands, opportunities, and threats flow into the "inbox" endlessly. I could spend unlimited time on each of the responsibilities to be a great teacher, researcher, networker, and administrator. Colleagues send emails around the clock. I must manage the intense time demands of this kind of work in a very personal way, with only myself to blame if I fail. It's like this for many workers. We each have only 168 hours a week. Some of those must be spent on the fact that we are *human beings*, not *human doings*. Our physical, social, spiritual selves must be fed on all levels – or we will die. Yet modern paid work relentlessly ignores these demands. We adjust on the private side: we avoid or postpone children, we import workers to care for our dependents, we relocate worldwide for work and thereby strain kinship networks and place-based identities, we eat on the run, lose sleep, and forget to exercise. We forget how to breathe deeply, turn off and tune in. We fill empty spaces with busy consumption. We rarely question the work, instead we blame ourselves for failing. What do these changes say about the way work is fitting into, or taking over, our lives?

We're living through a work situation that continues the values of the industrial revolution in the context of a technology revolution that detaches work from time and place limits, with not-always-healthy consequences for human beings. The physical, social, and spiritual needs of the human being had been built into the fabric of society historically. Every culture set aside days for rest and celebration, valued and regulated relations between and among people, made arrangements for the care of the next generation and of the elderly. Some things are supposed to happen as part of being human, but these fall outside of modern commodified understandings of *work* and have lost their legitimate place in the idealized contemporary modern workday, work week. Or life.

Implications for Work Design

There are actually four kinds of work, all vital. First there's *paid work*, these days acting like the king, taking his tax in the form of the prime waking hours and years, defining social identity, defined by male life courses, and increasingly greedy, leaving ever-fewer crumbs for the others. The second is *unpaid work*, keeping self and surroundings clean, maintained, cared for: Cinderella, slaving away invisibly, but whose absence is evident if she goes off to dance with – or become – the king. The third kind is *kinkeeping work*, maintaining family relations, work often not acknowledged as work at all, but if it doesn't happen, then the support networks will not be there in the event of emergency or to remind us of our humanity. The fourth kind of work is *education*, formally assigned to the young but vital for the mind's longevity. *Sustainable work design* will make space for all four and recognize that human beings need also to recharge and reconnect with themselves, need space outside of *work*.

Thus some of our rising productivity must be used for buying back our lives, not for increasing financial returns. Time and task management over the life course and across gender divides are crucial public issues. It's a waste of human resources to divide work as we currently do. Dividing the work so that men primarily do the *kingly* paid work hurts men's and children's health; having women specialize in *Cinderella* unpaid and kinkeeping work increases women's risks of poverty and deprives paid work spheres of women's talents. Assuming that all education must occur before age 25 or 30 bankrupts society by warehousing potential talent in unemployment. Let's invest in education all along the life course, allow ebbs and flows in work biographies, invite everyone to all four kinds of work, and leave space for life outside of work, for *free space*.

Future Work and How Neoliberal Ideology Is Taking Over

Stella Fleischer

Ever since the 1930s when the new liberal idea came into existence, it has had a tough job. But public and scientific denouncement has not been nearly as severe as it has been in recent years which has seen the call for a new social order that punishes the culture of dependency and appeals to people's initiative, self-reliance and self-determination, in other words, to ongoing, self-motivated activity. What has come under fire the most is the consistent and radical market economy orientation, the liberal economic policy and the increasing subjugation of the people's working and living environments to the market and its imperatives of efficiency and competition.

In any case, even when the economic system is on the verge of collapsing, these principles, which serve prosperity and progress, still remain in place. They match a social character that has always been the engine of any economy and economic growth: the entrepreneur. This heroic figure with *superhuman powers* is essential for modern capitalist societies. Not surprisingly, in the course of the hegemony of neoliberalism, entrepreneurs or entrepreneurial activity became a social and political guide. This was a clever move: an entrepreneur is a dazzling figure with many qualities, but he is also characterized by a certain homelessness and lack of commitment. Adaptability and risk appetite are other ways to describe him and suggest that he is ideally suited for a flexible, de-standardized, pluralized and boundless working system.

But the competencies required to become an entrepreneur do not arise just like that. They need special stimuli which are found at a systemic-structural, an institutional and at an individual level and which should socialize each worker so that they can socialize themselves in terms of their marketability. Today's workers and those of the future have to be ready and willing to actualize, reproduce and offer their working capabilities automatically. The challenge here is to be on *standby*, to be willing; the separation of labor and capital has lapsed, and each worker is his own asset. But does this only concern (future) workers? Where will the willingness for self-optimization and desire to be attractive for the market come from? The thesis is that the development of the productive forces and thus personnel development begins at school and is functional for the post-Fordist regime of accumulation and the capital's demand. One might conclude that the Marxist principle of the dialectic of the development of the productive forces and production conditions in various neo-liberalisms is being discussed today more than ever before.

Indications for the dominance of the neo-liberal trio *liberalization – privatization – deregulation* in the working system have already been cited. But what has appeared to be the emancipation from incrusted bureaucracy is really a qualitative new and comprehensive form of subjugation to market principles and, on the individual level, it promotes appropriate self-exploitation and self-responsibility. But even the educational system is under the auspices of neo-liberal principles and rationality. The educational system, the Bologna-Process or the manifold benchmarks and rankings within schools of general and higher education all underscore the assumption that market principles have been transferred to non-economic fields. These structural tendencies are equivalent to changes and tendencies both on a content level and on an individual level. Shifts in the curriculum and competence coupled with the growing number of initiatives for student-enterprises are more indications.

Thus neo-liberal ideology and principles took up increasingly more room and became dominant – Gramsci would call it hegemonic. What we are witnessing here is that common modes of governing and governmental rationality are changing from being despotic or authoritarian, like repressive physical pressure or violent disciplining to *liberal,* participatory, cooperative and self-determined governmental modes. The neo-liberal governmentality (Foucault) operates on the premise of *the conduct of conduct* and supplements forms, strategies and techniques to wield power over human behavior and life in the sense of political regulation as well as to guide the way in which an individual conducts himself (*techniques of the self*).

If the educational system is infiltrated by neo-liberal ideas, this will have far-reaching implications for future work and the employment system. Schools not only have a mandate to educate. They are also a place where important foundations for entrepreneurial thinking and practice are laid and where individuals acquire those skills suitable for individual and social reproduction. The neo-liberal imperatives of self-responsibility and self-activation are mediated by educational institutions intended to prepare manpower for the demands of the employment world. This requires making future workers responsible for themselves, their lives, intellectual capital and health and creates the willingness to be both employable and attractive for the new capitalist economy. We have to be particularly vigilant especially with regard to individual health and the psycho-physical adaptation to economic calculus.

In my view, the future of work and employment can only be assessed by using an integrative approach which includes the educational system and its importance for the systematic production of manpower. Failure to do this constitutes an inadmissible shortfall which will become quite apparent when using the concept of *lifelong learning,* for instance.Learning does not simply start with the entry into the workforce. So, if there is a crucial need to create an *entrepreneurial self* and to 'interpellate' the worker wholeheartedly with all his subjectivity and personality, then educational institutions cannot be excluded because this is where the foundation will be laid.

The Future Lies Somewhere in Between

Barbara Light

The future is bright. Or it is the *end of history* as we know it. Or it is whatever we choose to make of it and depends on collective envisioning...

If you were to say that the future is bright to the many people who have recently lost or are in the process of losing their jobs or are even long-term unemployed or underemployed (currently 2.65 million unemployed in the UK and rising), they would look at you as if you had stepped off a spaceship from another planet. How can the future possibly be bright in the midst of the worst recession in most people's living memories? Can't you see we have no money, no job, and no prospects? Where were you during the August 2011 riots when cities burned across the UK and looters carried away goods from smashed shops? And what about the cuts to welfare and public services that will adversely affect our quality of life? And the 1 in 5 young employed – our 'lost' generation? So is the future dire for these people? Are we at the end of an era that we are still clinging to, thus failing to recognize the opportunities and the innovations we could set in motion?

The Crisis of Capitalism

These are critical questions that we are all facing – certainly in the developed western world. The system of globalized capitalism seems to have created the mess we are now in, so how can we emerge and create a brighter future for ourselves and our world? Capitalism is not homogeneous – there are different types operating in geographically and culturally diverse parts of the globe. While unchallenged fundamentally liberal left/right ideologies are at the core of all the socio-economic political systems in the developed western countries, differences are prevalent in the extent of the provision of welfare and distribution of wealth. However, one thing is clear – there is a crisis of the system, and a lack of clarity on what to replace it with.

Some analysts point to the fact that capitalism is a volatile system with inherent tendencies to crises that are shifted both geographically and in form. This can be seen in examples such as the labor crisis in the 1970's, which was solved by changing the nature of work – from national manufacturing and service bases to global off-shoring. In many countries, particularly in the US and the UK, easy credit was extended to people so that they could consume despite no real increases in their wages. Property and land crises have occurred since then, for example, in Japan. The current crisis is one of capital, of delusion, and of greed: markets such as derivatives or carbon trading have been created to allow major investments, but these are invented assets. Political and national capital is being spent on shoring up failing financial systems – including the Euro! All in all, not a reassuring picture.

In the UK, contrary to ideological belief, government spending as a proportion of aggregate growth has actually decreased over the past 30 years, while consumption-particularly in areas such as recreation and communications-has risen substantially. Some reports have highlighted that particular sectors of the economy such as services, high tech, and low carbon resources could construct the future through building on emerging opportunities. Innovative ideas in any sector cannot be predicted; however, it is critical that contextual pre-conditions are established to allow innovation. These conditions should be enabled by government policies that fund and support innovation: from study and research and innovation hubs to direct support to companies that innovate – recognizing that these can hold a significant key to a revived economic future. Interconnectedness between diverse stakeholders (including understanding where customer demand will come from) also needs to increase as a pre-condition to facilitate a positive spiral of innovation – and this should be global, not national.

No More Woolly Vests

Companies themselves need to make a paradigmatic shift from autocratic models that control tasks and people to models that enable and empower people, and, critically, encourage creative dissent. Such an approach, however, demands new skills for the workforce who will be able to use and to innovate technology effectively and create new and sustainable opportunities benefitting themselves, their multiple organizations and the wider world. These entrepreneurial or agile people with flexible, intra-professional portfolios of knowledge, skills and experiences are also being termed 'liquid' workers, who move fast, learn fast, use new business models such as crowd-funding, crowd-sourcing and barter, and are not afraid to step into untested domains.

Liquidity also has a sustainable side to it, which would echo with a 'green' vision of the future. Ask a committed 'green' what the future will look like, and they will talk about small, local enterprises for work, energy and food provision, and shared transport systems. They will also tell you about bartering and about 'make do and mend' where our throw-away consumer goods can be re-used, mended and recycled and where manual work returns to its pre-industrial/technological revolution pre-eminence.

In my view, the future of work lies somewhere in between: yes, the global capitalist system needs a significant overhaul that shifts from greed and its current 'extreme' incarnation to one that *serves* humanity and works *with* our natural world. Yes, technological developments will continue at speed, and we should harness them to work more flexibly and learn continuously. Yes, we need new and sustainable business models and low carbon energy, but surely we do not need to return to woolly vests and hand-ploughing?

So change is needed at all levels – but we should embrace the future, innovate it, and not crawl backwards!

Human Workforce

The Return of the Human

Thomas Wallner

We somehow forgot that business economics is a branch of social sciences. Despite all the assertions that economics is actually all about people, the very nature of human beings has hardly been recognized – in particular in the way we organizc work. As things turn more complex and trivial approaches fail, this may change.

Human Work and Human Nature

Of course, work has always been human work. It has not always been humane though. Paid labor and in particular industrial work always bore connotations of exploitation, alienation and oppression. This was – besides all factual economic hardship endured by the working class – due to the fact that work was to its greater part machine-like and machine-dominated. As such, work is composed of externally controlled repetitive executions based on the division of labor. It is specialized, simplified and standardized. This organizational concept named Taylorism (after Frederick Winslow Taylor) follows a hierarchical command and control approach. Thinking and controlling is separated from the doing of the work. The individual contribution of the worker is hardly detectable in the final product. Often the worker does not even know what the final product is.

This is the nature of industrial work as it has mostly been organized, described, depicted and criticized for more than a century up to now. And, as many say, it does not comply with human nature. This has also been the predominant organizational paradigm for industrial companies (and not only for those; in fact this is the foundation of scientific management). For cost effective mass production, the Taylorist model was most successful. Still, in this deterministic, cost-oriented world, human work was under constant threat to be replaced. Too slow, too failure-prone, too imprecise, too unreliable and in particular too expensive – that's what human work is, making it the prime target for streamlining and automation measures.

However, in the past decades, we have seen a fast changing world, due to globalization, technological progress and ever increasing economic interconnectedness. Short product life cycles, mass customization, the volatility of markets on the demand and the supply side impose extraordinary challenges on organizations in terms of flexibility, resilience and innovativeness. The terms usually used to describe these environments we live and work in today are *dynamic*, *diverse*, *interdependent*, or most often, *complex*. Now, complexity is not what you would want to tackle with deterministic measures. Consequently, those traveling on the taylorist shore try to *reduce* complexity, which means in fact that they build a model with reduced options. The problem is that you cannot navigate in volatile fast changing environments based on a standardized set of responses.

What we need today is smart, real-time decision making based on weak signals and dynamic fuzzy goals. We must detect patterns fast and respond based on scarce information with a limited set of resources. We have to adapt continuously, which means that we have to learn continuously as individuals and as organizations. And more often than not, we have to come up with something new. We need these abilities on all levels of the organization, not only in the high ranks. Interesting enough, humans are good at that. Humans are designed to deal with complexity. We are built for the jungle. We are not built for the Taylorist circus. We are not good at skillfully repeating the same empty routine over and over again.

Human beings are open, living systems. As such we are purposeful and self-organizing; we can learn, adapt, and create. We can change ends and means under constant conditions, which does not only exemplify free will but is also a prerequisite for any innovation of disruptive quality.

Intuition, smart heuristics, dynamic self-organization to fulfill our own purpose or to pursue a *commander's intent* individually or as a team–to name a few of the ingredients–allow for fast, flexible and intelligent acting from a holistic perspective which cannot be matched by a Taylorist organization.

Implications for Work Design

At the University of Applied Sciences Upper Austria, we explore the role of human aspects in supply networks. In our research cooperation with manufacturing companies, we have identified a growing interest in and a rising demand for this specific distributed *shop-floor intelligence*.

One particular approach in this regard – and the focus of our scientific work – are high-performance work systems. High performance work systems provide a conceptual framework for organizing work in a way that effective self-organization can take place. They comprise particular management practices concerning organization of work and of the company itself, such as self-managed teamwork, job rotation, flat hierarchical structures, performance-related wages, or workforce empowerment. They focus on continuous reinvention processes of products and services, integrating creativity, experience and implicit knowledge of employees at all levels resulting in a new appreciation of human work. There is ample empirical evidence on their impact with regard to higher productivity, stronger financial performance, increased organizational agility, and innovativeness. Thus they are considered to contribute substantially to the generation of sufficient competitive advantage to keep manufacturing domestic despite high labor costs. By the same token, they show higher job satisfaction and a reduction of perceived workload, which will be of increasing importance in the future to attract new talent.

High-performance work systems are just one example among many other ideas and concepts. There is great untapped potential in acknowledging the fundamentals of human nature for the co-design of work and collaboration, and there is more to come.

The Rebirth of Guilds – Restoring the Social Fabric of Our Communities

Charlie Grantham

Guilds as a form of social organization for craftsmen emerged in Europe in the 13th century. They originated as a way to provide social support to skilled workers so economic forces would not exploit them, and to protect their "secret knowledge." Wherever specialized skill and knowledge accumulated, these associations were formed to focus and organize the practice of their craft. They related to the larger economy, as they were places where young people went to learn a trade, find work and, we would assume, a supportive social network.

Industrialization and capitalism supplanted the need for guilds through concurrent development of public education, work specialization and routinization of work tasks. Guilds began to lose influence and disappear as a philosophy of "free trade" and laissez-faire economic theory moved to the forefront.

There are several forces, which pave the way of organizing talent pools. We feel four of them are driving the rebirth of guilds.

Failure of Industrial Institutions

Without a doubt, the institutions which served humanity well in the industrial era have reached the end of their useful life. Just as feudalism fell away with the Enlightenment, and royalty with the rise of the modern nation-state, the same applies for industrial capitalism, tribal governments and supporting establishments.

Technology Speeds up Education and Continuous Learning

Technology, especially when it influences how we *communicate* with each other, causes a change in our sense and experience *of time and space*. This change, in turn, brings about a change in our *mental energy* (or how we pay attention to things) and this finally results in a change in *our behavior*.

Search for Community that Is Intimate

It is hard to argue against the rise of a sense of need for community around the planet. Community is the social glue that holds everything together, gives people hope, and provides them with a psychological anchor in times of trouble.

Devolution of Power

We contend that political power is devolving from massively centralized structures to a loosely knit network of community federations. During the Middle Ages, government and religion were intertwined. Underlying all of this regulation and control lies a belief system that is agreed-upon and shared. When belief structures change, eventually so does the governance structure. And at this point in human history, these beliefs are changing once again.

The basic structure of work behavior is changing. Our society (at least in the developed world) is moving away from an industrial model to a community-based model, which strangely resembles how we organized ourselves – before the Industrial Revolution. Specially organized groups known as guilds exercised control over economic life in the Middle Ages. The essential purpose of guilds was to create monopolies. They tried to exclude from the local market, to the extent possible, both the outside trader and the independent trader inside who was not a member of the guild. These early organizations represent only a beginning. If flexible working arrangements of various sorts become even more common in the future, we will need much more extensive ways of meeting human needs.

These guilds could provide a stable home for their members as they move from job to job. They could, for example, help their members by:

- Ensuring their financial security,
- Providing placement and professional training services,
- Becoming a locus of social interaction and identification.

Guilds appear to be an especially promising way of addressing two challenges. First, by providing insurance and pensions, professional development and placement programs, and access to a social milieu, guilds can allow workers to take advantage of flexible employment relationships without having to face high risks and unattractive social repercussions. Second, by emphasizing continuous learning for their members and the matching of workers' skills with available opportunities.

Return to Guilds – Some Implications

This new approach has the potential to radically change the terms of debates that have been central to the industrial age. Today collective bargaining is a primary role of many unions, and we typically assume that the interests of unions and management will be in conflict. In a world of flexible networks of one-person companies, there would often be no stable centralized management to bargain with.

A return to guilds as an organizing force for the worker of the future will bring with it another medieval institution: a return of the ownership in the means of production to the individual. As technology has become commoditized, individuals can afford to own the fastest, latest and most robust equipment. No longer must workers depend on their employer to give them the tools they need to do their job. The industrial model has been that companies provide workers with everything they need to do the job: office space, technology, and management support – including health care, pensions and training. But guilds will provide all that for workers.

When our scenario plays out, companies will find themselves in the envious position of shedding the responsibility of providing human resource services, technology infrastructure and facilities. You could literally cut your operational expenses in half for 30–40% of the workforce. What's the dark side for companies and what will they have to do to counteract loosening their social ties with workers? In short, their death. Loosening these community's ties implies a growing lack of engagement between worker and companies. These companies have historically existed to find, organize and focus the energy and talent of people who add value in the process of innovation, manufacture and distribution of goods and services. Some form of human organization will be required to step in and fill that gap: guilds.

Working in the Latin American Jaguar: The Crucial Role of Trade Unions

Patrizio Tonelli

In Chile, the development and transformation of work are related to a clearly defined phenomenon: *the precarization and weakening of work's collective action chances.* Despite a very positive macroeconomic performance that has received international recognition, people are accessing work in temporary and precarious ways without having real opportunities to take part in the wealth they produce and in the decisions regarding their conditions. The future of work should ideally reverse this situation and focus on the quality of work. In order to do this, we should focus our attention on building up a *strong labor and industrial relations system* that is fully able to place work and its requirements at the center of a productive system.

Quality of Work: A Focus on Chilean Labour Market

Chile has been called the "Latin American Jaguar" for its macroeconomic performance which is unparalleled on the rest of the continent. Based on a production structure that consists of the extraction and export of natural resources and the expansion of commercial activities such as supermarkets, Chile has grown strongly in recent years posting a $15,000 (USD) GDP per capita and the best regional productivity rates. Last, but not least, between January 2010 and November 2011 the government welcomed the creation of 576,000 jobs which significantly cut the unemployment rate to below 7%. This data might lead the reader to conclude that work is thriving in Chile and that it is a place of job creation and self-realization.

The reality, however, is totally different.

For a few years now, the Fundación SOL (SOL Foundation) has been analyzing monthly employment and labor market data provided by the Chilean National Institute of Statistics (INE). The findings highlight a reality marked by high levels of insecurity.

The 576,000 new jobs can be broken down as follows:

- 49% of the jobs relate to self-employment, domestic staff and microentrepreneur (less than 5 employees). Employment here shows a high incidence of part-time and low-skilled jobs and does not include professional freelances or solid enterprises.
- 51% of the jobs are wage work (289,000 people) generated mostly through outsourcing and labor delivery which is an indication for precarious and unstable occupations.

In this context, Fundación SOL has drawn up a "labor market insertion index" which divides Chilean population in terms of its relationship to and integration in the labor market. Through this index we arrived at *3 concentric rings*. The first one is the "high insertion ring" which forms the core with formal, safe, continuous and steady employment. The second is the "average insertion ring" where we find a certain degree of job protection. The third is the "low insertion ring" which accounts for informal, unprotected and unstable jobs. Data shows that between January 2009 and November 2011, the *first ring declined and the third ring is the only one which increased* due to high incidences of "underemployed self employment" (people who want to work more hours but can't find the opportunity). Another interesting factor that points to the flexibilization and precarization process is the increasing number of part-time jobs inside the first ring.

This data tells us that the Chilean population is more frequently living in unprotected and weak working conditions, where, for example, low wages are the norm: 76% of wage earners earn less than $350.000 (CHP) net per month, an amount that doesn't permit a decent standard of living in Chile.

Decentralized Collective Bargaining

The main reason for this situation is linked to the unions and collective bargaining conditions which allow workers to actively participate in the establishment of quality jobs. Chile has low unionization levels (13.9%) and an extremely decentralized collective bargaining structure which only exists at the firm level. Chile therefore has a very low collective bargaining coverage rate (11%), meaning that a mere 11 out of 100 workers negotiate their working conditions, a situation that denotes absolute unilateralism and the inability to take part in work-related decisions. This leads to a disproportionate level of inequality.

At the same time, the only *business innovations* allowing participation and employee satisfaction are put forth by attraction strategies designed by HR management along the lines of "happy company" or "happiness management" models. Although the unilateral delivery of "emotional wages", prizes, individual benefits and propaganda encourage *the illusion* of creating a better job, they hinder the sound explanation of work's requirements and block any opportunity to influence working conditions. Basically, these models choose to ignore the evidence that work is a collective sphere which relies on autonomous collective interests, an element that should be the foundation of a change in our policies.

The Future of Work at the Crossroad

Ultimately, Chilean working conditions demonstrate that the future of work now stands at the crossroads. If we want to promote the quality of work, we should foster the collective bargaining capability of workers and revamp the labor relation system to give employees the chance to outline and value their real needs and potentials. In this way, work will recover its original meaning of self-realization and participation in social wealth. On the contrary, precarization and poverty will be its main features, transforming work into an oppressive machine for the majority of the population.

Psychological Health in Future Labor Markets – a Dystopia

Lena Hünefeld and Larissa Müller

The dark side of a not so distant future...

Humankind has been identified as a weak link within the production process. Humans' emotionality and concomitant susceptibility to psychological illnesses pose a high risk to the productivity of the world of employment. Therefore businesses have decided to substitute in robots and machines for humans whenever possible in the work process. The expulsion of people from the working environment leads to social relations that are characterized by unemployment and criminality.

In 2012, a rapid increase in reports of mental illnesses was recorded already; especially burnout presents a frequent work-related risk. Advanced globalization and individualization repeatedly challenged companies to develop innovative ideas to withstand international pressure and succeed economically. This had far-reaching consequences on the working conditions of employees: time pressure, long working hours, decreased job security, growing demands for flexibility and mobility. Employees have been increasingly overwhelmed with these conditions and felt stressed. This in turn led to companies' rising financial losses due to high absenteeism and frequent turnover based on psychological illnesses.

Dystopia

In the coming years, the situation in the labor market will visibly take a turn for the worse. Employees are indentured to their employers for 24 hours a day. Apart from their presence at the workplace, constant availability and mobility is demanded. This isolates employees from their social environment. Opportunities to reduce stress during leisure time are mostly non-existent. In addition, competition at the workplace is not limited to other employees and productivity but extends also to machines and robots. Everyone is at risk of being replaced by another worker or by a machine. Only those who can withstand the productivity demands without emotional costs or risking psychological illness can prevail in the labor market.

As part of these developments, additional mental illnesses other than burnout will emerge and Karoshi syndrome, death from overwork which was until 2012 restricted to Japan, will spread worldwide. Due to these new diseases, people will not only cease to be able to function properly, they will no longer be able to live. In addition, overextended employees will commit suicide out of desperation or go on killing sprees in companies, claiming additional lives. To avoid losses in productivity caused by emotionally overtaxed or mentally ill employees and to prevent rampages, companies regularly conduct psychological evaluations of their employees. Employees only gain access to the company or keep their employment if they pass these. The psychological resilience of an employee is a crucial element of the psychological assessment. This development will lead to the removal of a majority of people from the working world. Society will consequently be split into people that are declared mentally unstable and into people belonging to a select, psychologically stable elite that in turn controls the access to employment. The emotional life and, as a consequence, the human factor will be excluded as much as possible from the working world. The majority of humankind will be stigmatized as unproductive and therefore demoted to second class citizenry. For this group of people access to legal ways of earning money will be denied and they will continue to struggle to survive.

Implications for Work Design

To prevent the dystopia described, human individuals have to be recognized as valuable resources for the working process, and their emotionality as well as their creative potential has to be held in higher regard. People and their emotionality, for the most part, cannot be replaced in the working world; their expulsion should not be the objective. Emotionality should be recognized as strength at work. This human attribute is a source of motivation and identification within the work field. The ability to connect positive emotions with the job heightens motivation and contentment of employees. Emotions enable them to critically analyze work situations and to identify clients' wishes. The working conditions play an important role in the development of positive emotions towards work. Employees should be allowed to work autonomously, and they have to get the opportunity to perform meaningful work that represents a challenge. Furthermore, employers should facilitate a healthy coexistence of social and work life for employees and support them in realizing their personal and their professional goals. Day care should be offered by employers as well as options for employees to arrange their working hours flexibly.

Working processes should be humane and should not push the boundaries of psychological endurance. Employers should lead primarily with their employees' best interest in mind, reduce the pressure on their workforce, and allow strategic leisure and recovery time. Health-promoting measures can counteract stressful work situations. The increased use of disability managers is advisable. Their task would be detecting mental problems among employees and offering individual solutions to Management to keep their employees mentally healthy. The psychological evaluations mentioned in the dystopia could instead be used for employees' benefit. Regular assessments and their results could be utilized by companies to provide support for their employees. Similarly, disability managers should assist employees with mental illnesses. Additionally, a buddy-system should be introduced focusing on mutual support between colleagues in maintaining psychological health. Within this system, coworkers would pay attention to one another's unhealthy attitudes and talk about the problems they see in their behaviors. A better connection between the educational system and the world of work is essential to optimize the preparation of future employees. Moreover, trade unions, supervisory boards, and Works Councils should increasingly make sure that companies do not emotionally exploit their employees.

Risks and Side Effects of Knowledge-Intensive Work

Frank Striewe and Markus G. Schwering

The End of the Universal Resource Participation as a Strain Buffer

Although the issue *Prethinking Work* primarily refers to the future prospects of work, the past and the present of labor should also be considered. The question "Why do laborers work?" that was discussed during the industrial era will still remain relevant in the future. Kurt Lewin, who was one of the most fervent critics of Taylorism, already had a firm opinion about the role of work, "Labor is an indispensable requirement for living, however, it is not real life. [...] As you do not live in order to eat, but you eat in order to live; you work unavoidably so as to live, but you do not live so as to work." However, the answer to the question of the purpose and necessity of labor in the present and future, especially in terms of knowledge-intensive, high-level participative forms of working, is far more complex.

From the point of view of industrial psychology, participation has been regarded as the key element of human and personality-enhancing work organization for a long time. Meanwhile empirical results indicate that there is a series of problems that particularly affect employees of knowledge-intensive work forms with a high degree of participation. We therefore predict the end of the *universal resource* participation as a strain buffer and attempt an outlook on the consequences of work organization and design in sustainable organizations.

Rethinking Participation and Strain

The use of knowledge and the activation of employees' learning potential are considered to be the key to securing companies' long-term competitive advantages. Against this background, participative planning considerations will be much more center-stage in the context of ergonomic studies. While there is at least a programmatic consensus on the positive effects of participative work forms in science and practice, the effects of participative management in knowledge-intensive work forms have only recently and sporadically become an issue. Catch phrases such as the *dissolution of boundaries*, *subjectivization of work* and *work-life-balance* are often used in ergonomic research when discussing the risks and side effects of knowledge-intensive work forms. Regarding the connection between participation and strain in knowledge-intensive work forms, it has become clear that participation as a strain buffer has become less important. Isolated empirical findings support the assumptions of new practically concepts, according to which participation in knowledge-intensive work forms neither functions as a buffer against strain, nor does it have relief effects. In fact, there is a risk that individual employees overwork or get bogged down in contradictory working requirements, due to extensive participation margins. Although one positive result may be that the subjective work-oriented requirements and needs of the employees in knowledge-intensive work forms can be realized more easily. Nevertheless, a shifting of the relation between professional and daily life can be observed. This seems to negatively affect the subjective life-oriented requirements and needs.

These negative consequences are still tabooed by many companies. When, for example, an employee suffers burnout, a *lack of mental resilience*, *incompetence* and *poor leadership skills* are regarded as the cause of this illness. If companies and/or their responsible leaders respond to these developments, then mostly only by introducing behavioral measures such as strain-immunization training, time management exercises and management-training programs, etc. In addition, these measures will only be introduced after the consequences of harmful actions have already affected situational perception and assessment. Such an approach is based on the assumption that defined personality traits are responsible for a person's state of health.

Many companies still do not regard the creation of an appropriate structural and situational framework as well as resources for employees in the work context as one of their responsibilities. One consequence for the prospective work organization is: Restriction on dissolution of boundaries.

Work Design beyond Negative Strains

What will matter, in the future, is avoiding to place negative strain on employees, providing behavioral adjustments and creating work practices that enable employees to behave in a healthier way. Consequently, operational commitment should not be restricted to the use of behavioral instruments like *self-management courses* and *stress management programs*. It would be essential to focus on developing better general working conditions (e.g. socially acceptable work hours, operational guidelines for extra hours, influence of operational cultures regarding self-conception and work technique). In addition, efforts to establish a more effective balance between private and work life, which have already taken place, will have to be extended further. When designing knowledge-intensive work forms, it is no longer adequate to only expand the scope of decisions and operations. Instead, the focus should be on the contrary: The employees' degree of freedom should be restricted by institutionally anchored forms of self-organization and regulation. As a result, it would be possible to avoid the risks and side effects of knowledge-intensive work in the future.

Collective Competence

Rethinking the Future of Work – Some Thoughts

Leif Edvinsson

In a scenario that dates back to 1982, Peter Russell described world connections as a global brain of nodes. This description might be even more valid today where knowledge work is becoming more globally intcgrated through networks. Just look at the rapid growth of Facebook, which today numbers some 700 million users. In 2015, there will be an estimated 5 billion brains connected via broadband. What will be the implications for the future of work?

Recently at CES 2012 in Las Vegas, the CEO of Ericsson demonstrated an intelligent tree based on electronic sensors with small rapid communication chips of 4 G that are linked via mobile broadband stations. He explained how they have been investing in building the global broadband infrastructure and so-called Networked Society. He went on to say that the huge annual R&D investment is not really appreciated by the stock market, despite the fact that it contributes to a tremendous sustainable earning infrastructure in the exponentially growing Digital Future. Today's figure of 1 billion broadband users is estimated to grow to 5 billion in less than 5 years. According to their research, a 10% growth in broadband adds 1% to the GDP, and for every 1000 new broadband connections there will be 80 new network jobs. New structures will emerge where the value cooperative or work is in the Networked Innovative society and outside the realms of old enterprises and institutions. In most countries in Africa, 80% of the population has access to mobile phones, but only 25% to traditional banks. So, therefore new hybrids are emerging, such as telebanking.

Change of Mind and Values

The future of work depends on our ability to change our thinking. We will have to get used to the idea of searching for a Mindbox instead of a Toolbox and to link minds to minds to gain a deeper understanding of this emerging integrated thought system. We need to learn to think in a new way and to be in another consciousness based on connectivity, complexity and contactivity. We will need new job roles for the refined awareness and new training programs for the non-linear interactive roles. Robert Reich once highlighted the importance of the role of Symbol Analyst, a kind of Knowledge Navigator. For this, a deeper understanding of Intellectual Capital might be of help. Human capital will be amplified by leveraging organizational capital and borderless relational capital on a global scale. A part of this involves innovative contracting models for value creation. Just look at how Apple is leveraging individual innovators and is channeling this through the platform of App stores with enormous and rapid multiplication in volume, revenues and financial value.

A shift of values will occur in favor of the more effective and efficient interplay of community and individuality to make way for the upcoming potential of generations, such as Social Entrepreneurship, Community Banking, Creative Commons and Pentahelix systems beyond the simple Triple Helix model with proactive volunteers and new NGOs. In some societies, the issue of gender will be very transformative. Just look at the success of micro credits from the Grameen Bank or the program called Hand in Hand with now 700,000 female-based SMEs. These two major cases out of Asia are examples for engaging female talent to create wealth in developing economies. The future of work will need to find ways to engage female talent to benefit new kinds of social entrepreneurship and societal entrepreneurship, to name a few examples.

The Future of Collaborative and Open Innovation

Could there be yet another eco system like that of a living organism? What is the nervous system of our civilization? Human cells are becoming connected to humanity and a new human consciousness is emerging as a mental evolution where wisdom is reinforcing itself very similar to the algorithm of Google translate. Around 10 billion atoms might be the critical mass for an evolutionary step to the next level, according to Peter Russel. The human population is approaching this, but so is the volume of digital devices. This integration has also resulted in more and more so-called ‘open innovations’. The enterprise system and institutionalized work will be challenged. In more academic terms: the critical issue is to avoid institutional failure and bureaucracy by working on organizational innovations, for example, the Business Recipe innovation. Often this goes hand in hand with a new and energizing ecosystem with a knowledge flow, an in-sourcing of cross disciplinary perspectives and intelligence, cross-fertilizing skill and expertise. Cloud Computing and Social Media will play a greater and more powerful role for the new societal fabric. Just consider the case of the Arab Spring.

This is just the beginning, not only in Europe, but also around the globe. So where do we find the most innovative systems design not only for enterprise innovation, but also urban renewal, political renewal, financial currency renewal, youth engagement and social security innovations? OISPG (Open Innovation Strategy and Policy Group) has been pioneering many perspectives, initiatives and reports about work done on Open Innovation in an effort to enlighten and inspire prototyping projects. We need spaces that offer fail-safe environments for interacting and prototyping like the growing number of Future Centres, once started by Skandia, and now called, among others, Mindlab, Dialogue House, Multiversity, Living Labs etc.

The outlook and insights for a collective rapid learning of these emerging signals might be one of the most important perspectives and items of the Vision and Agenda 2020 for Innovative Europe. The risks lie in not detecting, understanding and acting for continuous renewal due to ignorance. So out of the growing problems of institutional failure, the emerging power of the digital work space will offer fresh new opportunities. We are already seeing how IT indicators and health indicators correlate over time with IC growth and societal wealth. How rapidly will established institutions and enterprises both public and private be ready to proactively respond to such challenges…?

Competence in Use – Project-Based Competence Nets to Organize Work

Christina Öberg

In an effort to create organizational flexibility and focus on competence in use, this chapter would like to propose project-based competence nets as one way of organizing work. The *project*-based organization is marked by its temporary nature: it exists while it performs its output and dissolves once the project is completed. The focus on *competencies* describes how individuals commit to the project because of their skills and their complementarity. The *net* as the organizational unit underlines that the competencies may not belong to the same company. Project-based competence nets are inspired by innovative companies (open-source software and crowd-sourcing), construction companies and advertising/web agencies.

The Need for Project-Based Competence Nets

The future work environment will require new ways of organizing work because of its focus on continuous change and the goal to keep administration to a minimum. The resourceful use of individual skills highlights project-based competence nets and the need to blend flexibility with the efficient use of competencies.

In research on networks, strategic alliances or joint ventures, the *net* has been increasingly emphasized as the organizational unit. Rather than referring to the company as the supplying party, the net is a group of companies that commits to a shared interest and delivers a joint output to customers. In essence, such nets have described sets of companies. Contracts among the companies point to them being a lasting unit. However, such nets may well be temporary (such as the construction site) and focus on individuals rather than companies as the contributing units (as in open-source software and crowd-sourcing). In its purest form, the project-based competence net consists of individuals that have complementary skills and abilities. Their competencies need to be bundled to make a customer offering. Rather than becoming part of a company, contributing individuals volunteer or have a temporary contract for pre-designed or co-designed tasks.

This emphasizes competence in use, i.e., how the net is organized so that those individuals who actually contribute their competencies are those that also participate. Competence in use further stresses that the individuals work at what they are most skilled to do and that the net optimizes the use of their competence and minimizes their efforts in other areas. Knowledge is accumulated by the contributing individuals and transferred between projects as they participate in new ones. The individuals are self-employed and driven by their own development, income level and the chance to interact with other parties in the projects who, in turn, enhance their own knowledge and contribute to the further development of their competencies.

Advantages and Obstacles

What are the advantages of project-based competence nets? The opportunities could be divided between organizational and customer-related (offering) areas. The work organization enables individuals to maintain their independence, to work based on their interests (issues that have been described as central for generations ahead) while at the same time drawing on each other's knowledge. This model minimizes the slack time between projects and the amount of administrative work. Each project also has the potential to attract those competencies which best fit the specific task and select among any number of individuals, not just those who belong to a specific company. Since new projects with new combinations of participants are continuously being formed, the output will be characterized by newness rather than repetition. As expected, the involvement of parties with different backgrounds and the project-basis for their interaction leads to an increase in creativity. For customers, the manner in which work is organized means that customized products and services are produced, and the customer may also volunteer as a project member to impact the outcome.

The greatest obstacle – but one which could hold out the prospect of an opportunity – is knowledge transfer. The nets facilitate the transfer of knowledge between projects based on how contributing individuals take part in new projects. However, the knowledge is in the hands of individuals and not of an organizational unit. To build on previous knowledge, the project needs to attract individuals that have accumulated such knowledge. This necessitates a mutual affinity between individuals and projects to make participation attractive. Efforts need to focus on marketing the project to the right participants.

Implications for Work Design

Without a doubt the project-based competence net has greater potential for businesses where customers require specific offerings each and every time. The nets are also more important when participants base their outputs on their competencies rather than on the equipment or ability to present working hours with a low level of flexibility or creativity in output. Innovations and creative work, such as advertising, architecture and high-tech companies are among those that benefit the most from this form of work organization. However, the project-based competence net could also inspire new ways of organizing businesses such as management consultancies, construction works and research and development departments. In fact, any business that needs new ideas, customized solutions, or that puts forth the competencies of individuals could consider this way of organizing work.

The benefits of the project-based competence net lie in flexibility, incorporation of customized competencies specific to the project and in its diversification. The competencies should not be too diverse, however, given that greater differences mean increased difficulties in understanding one another and working together. A balance needs to be achieved in terms of competencies and their complementarity and contributing powers. It is also important to create commitment among the contributing parties. While there may be written contracts for the projects, the contributing parties need to see their own benefit and commit to the shared efforts. Such a commitment is created, for instance, through interesting tasks and the involvement of individuals with attractive skills and abilities.

On Being One Innovative Professional Community

Gabriele Hoeborn and Jennifer Bredtmann

Up until now the success of the German economy has been mainly due to the innovative work of highly qualified specialized professionals, while the production of simpler products has been outsourced to countries with low production costs for efficiency reasons. Just a short while ago many highly specialized professionals like engineers or skilled workers received generous early retirement packages and were replaced by younger employees. Meanwhile, thousands of specialized and knowledgeable professionals in product development, for instance, are no longer in the workforce. At the same time, many studies on the skills and abilities of senior employees are being carried out. It turns out that older professionals are interested and willing to be a part of change a fact that points to the openness to learn, something that knows no bounds with regards to age or time limitations. It goes without saying that there is no place for age segregation or discrimination. A training culture has to be created that considers and supports different age-specific learning abilities and other aspects.

A First Approach to Solution

Certainly the pressure from the enormously competitive globalized economy on lifelong learning, on self-organized or even on self learning are factors that necessitate advanced training in any innovative company. In view of this, it is important to offer the necessary conditions to accommodate the individual learning requirements of each employee. A model which supports self-learning, in particular, can be used to train a specific target group. Participating senior employees feel appreciated, on the one hand, and, on the other hand, their individual learning styles are considered.

Self-organized learning can be applied through serious games. Compared to other self-organized lifelong learning tools, serious games are also the responsibility of the learners. The premise with them is that the learner is open to learning and the games boost the confidence through individual play. Because the games are adaptable, they can relate to future scenarios, and in personal way the learner absorbs the content of the serious game. The editors' personal experiences underscore the use of serious games as an appreciated and effective tool.

A holistic view on advanced training has to focus on individual learning skills and abilities as well as on individual learning strategies. Processes and methodologies have to be adapted to suit different requirements. Advanced education has to be anthropocentric. Combining mediation and self-learning by using, for instance, serious games to reduce learning conflicts and increase self-learning motivation is quite a new approach, and as yet there are only a few results for this target group.

From the standpoint of society, this also holds out the prospect of potential. The possibility for older, highly qualified specialized professionals to participate in a company's advanced training increases the competitiveness of companies and opens them up to global markets. Also, employment is secured and the working conditions for older professionals staying on in the company are improved. This sets change in motion. When there is a lack of highly qualified and specialized workers, satisfaction and identification with one's work is an important aspect to ensure innovation, ability and competitiveness.

Professional Community and Its Way to Form a Unified Whole

The role and position of older employees is defined by exclusion and by largely ignoring their experience and knowledge. This sort of age discrimination has to be replaced. It is quite possible that one innovative professional community may no longer be a sustainable vision; it has to be defined as a crucial and determining goal. There are four main issues which an innovative company has to tackle en route to becoming this community. Firstly, enterprises have to implement *creativity freedom* including a time and area as well as the necessary material. For economic reasons, there are time limitations, but there should be flexibility to be creative. Some companies have tried to realize comparable approaches, but the creative community has to involve all of the employees equitably. Secondly, creativity like any process of mutual development needs open and *critical discussions*; here discord is a must. The culture of crucial discussions has to be implemented as a part of the company philosophy and company culture. Therefore, thirdly, the formal and informal abilities and talents of employees have to be complied to implement *long-term training perspectives*. The company can set up a data base with this information and a panel can indicate requirements and current abilities of employees. Fourthly, the *economic evaluation* of a company should not consider its capital alone, but also the knowledge and abilities of employees. Informal abilities should also be included.

A company that proceeds in this manner can successfully offer further training and promote lifelong learning. All training measures have to be integrated into daily work processes to ensure sustainability. As self-reliant members of their community, employees can decide which training modules to choose from and when and how to tackle them. They need flexible tools that are independent of time and place and of individual user circumstances and conditions.

Tapping into the potentials and talents of all employees by incorporating everyone into the community and accepting the demands of all employees builds a company that performs well, that includes all members of its community and offers target groups specific training for lifelong learning.

The Fading Line between Working and Learning

Yvonne Salazar

Time to market of new products is continuously decreasing. Production processes change due to the introduction of value production systems, lean manufacturing, continuous improvement processes (CIP) and total productive maintenance (TPM). These developments, plus the increasing dynamics and turbulences of global markets, demand that companies be able to react quickly and decisively to changes in the market.

High performance companies are able to adapt flexibly to fluctuations in quantities, quality, time of delivery, varieties of products and costs in their production. To do so, they generate so-called flexibility corridors. So, should market sales rise suddenly, a third working shift is implemented or temporary workers are hired to cover the demand for increased production. As a result of the globalization of the economy, the factors influencing economic performance continue to grow in diversity, and become more and more dynamic and volatile. Unpredictable disasters, such as the nuclear accident at Fukushima, or a volcanic eruption, have an immediate impact on industrial production, due to a sudden lack of spare parts or raw materials. Consequently, standard corridors of flexibility are no longer sufficient. Changeability that encompasses the ability to react to the unforeseeable future in a proactive and anticipatory way has to be achieved. For this purpose new flexibility corridors need to be designed, analyzed and evaluated according to their economic feasibility or meaningfulness. A new flexibility corridor could be created, for example, by storing huge quantities of raw material or finished goods; however, some other choice may be more efficient and more economic. Alternative solutions have to be developed, simulated and evaluated for the "worst case" scenario. Thus, changeability is the potential to implement organizational and technological changes beyond existing flexibility corridor capabilities considering dimensions of adaptability, scalability, modifiability, and robustness.

Empower Staff to Change

Staff is often blamed for impeding change. They treat change skeptically or reject it entirely. Closely examined however, it becomes evident that staff is seldom involved in the shaping of change and that they are not given the freedom to select options. On the other hand, they are often not able to identify signals for the necessity of change, to evaluate them and to initiate the corresponding activities. In order to think in alternatives and new flexibility corridors, staff must be able to find their way in open, complex and dynamic situations in a self-organized way. They must have the skills needed to perceive changing environmental conditions and situations, to analyze them and derive consequences for their actions in the company and the resulting requirements for learning.

Implications for Work Design

Training to cope with the rapid and complex changes can hardly be outsourced to external training departments or academies as they can rarely cope with the transient, varying and highly specific training needs of a company. Moreover, the organizational conditions for learning are changing radically. The time available for learning is declining, while the need continues to grow. Learning has to be executed "just in time" and "on demand". Thus, training is yielding to new forms of learning and human resources development. Consequently,

- Short, quick training sequences and learning in and near the work process increase
- Learning processes are shifted from external offers to internal measures
- Managerial staff has to assume the role of coaches, and
- Colleagues become instructors/trainers.

New groups of employees will have to integrate learning into their professional duties and behavior. The complexity of challenges that have to be dealt with leads to the situation where, for example, management courses no longer target executive managers, but address shift coordinators, line managers and team leaders. Moreover, skills like flexibility or self-awareness cannot be developed by attending a training course. They have to be developed by different means of staff development like job rotation and job enrichment. For example, analytical skills can be fostered by creating weekly or monthly routines to evaluate the work flow and / or the problem of the week or month.

Measures that support the development of changeability are:

- Development of a feedback and continuous improvement culture
- Skill building workplace design
- Target group-oriented learning
- Learning networks.

In many cases, learning is not formalized, but takes place unnoticed. Informal learning in this context means that learning is not structured with regard to learning objectives, duration and design. It includes the chat during a break with colleagues over coffee, when we call the hotline or ask a colleague for advice or help. Informal learning cannot be ordered or monitored, but lies in the hands and minds of each individual. Information sharing and networking beyond the managerial level is an essential element of informal learning. Especially in the context of changeability, companies should consider the willingness of employees to coordinate themselves and to cooperate as a resource, and make active use of this collaboration. An *active learning culture* can and should be promoted by creating spaces for communication. The simplest options are coffee kitchens or small cafeterias where staff can meet and share ideas about work. A targeted promotion of workplace learning is the establishment of so- called "learning islands" that allow a team to come together and to discuss current issues, developments and experiences during the work process. If a corporate culture encourages and recognizes the value of information exchange and implicit learning, and fosters the sharing of knowledge, then changeability becomes an intrinsic characteristic resulting in a competitive edge.

In the future, workplace learning will have to increase in almost all industries. The challenge of changeability will foster the merger of working and learning, resulting in a fading line so that we will often hardly know if we are working or learning.

Working to Co-create New Functionality Beyond Economic Value

Kayano Fukuda

Value creation is today recognized as an important work goal. In a rapidly changing and uncertain world, sustainable value creation has significance for competitiveness and even survival of organizations as well as productivity of individuals. Sustainable value creation necessitates rethinking about the value to be created from a long-term perspective. Many organizations and individuals define value creation narrowly, and remain focused on economic value. Their primary concern is still to optimize short-term profit, not to address individual and community needs in a long perspective.

Economic value cannot be the only goal for society. Economic growth sometimes causes serious environmental destruction, and also widens social inequalities. Over the past decades, progress in manufacturing has made a significant contribution to economic development as well as the improvement of living standards. On the other hand, it heavily depended on raw materials and cheap energy, and consequently caused global climate change, loss of biodiversity and toxic contaminations. Modern capitalism also has increased the income gap and social stratification.

Work should balance economic growth with the progress and well-being of society. It must create value that will not only achieve economic success but also satisfy social, cultural, aspirational and emotional needs. Most organizations and individuals are still stuck in thinking that profit is the purpose of work. It is a big challenge for the future of work to change this mindset and go beyond economic value.

Co-creating New Functionality as New Option to Change Thinking

Creation of new functionality beyond economic value is one option to address this challenge. The principle of new functionality includes not only creating economic value but also satisfying broader expectations of society. While some organizations and individuals are endeavoring to create new functionality, more efforts are required to shift the focus of work from maximizing profits to social, cultural, aspirational and emotional needs. New functionality is not created by producers of innovative goods and services, but by producers and consumers together in a co-evolutionary way. Thus, co-creating new functionality will bring social welfare, cultural well-being, improvement of the standard of living and emotional satisfaction besides economic benefits.

Consumers in many countries have been more nervous about spending money after the global financial crisis in 2008. They have cut back on discretionary spending such as dining out and purchasing luxuries, and switched to cheaper products as the new normal. Japanese consumers have also been changing their lifestyle and awareness after the unprecedented triple disaster – the most powerful earthquake ever recorded, a massive tsunami and a meltdown at a nuclear power plant – on March 11, 2011. The nationwide efforts to deal with electricity shortages during the summer have improved awareness about energy conservation. People have been paying more attention to traditional ways to keep cool and warm as well as new ways to save and generate energy at home such as energy efficient appliances and photovoltaic systems. Experiences in the aftermath have also increased their perception of eliminating waste and ethical consumption with minimal exploitation of communities. These changes in consumer behavior imply that consumers more carefully examine benefits relative to cost from a perspective that is broader than the short-term and economic one.

The Next Wave of Innovation

Creation of new functionality could respond to such changes, and will drive the next wave of innovation in the modern working environment. In the past, innovation success depended on how producers delivered innovative goods and services. However, it now depends on how consumers value innovation outputs. Consumers are eager to share global best practices and develop new needs. Producers are expected to provide solutions for consumers' needs, whether identified, still hidden or potentially emerging. New functionality is emerged when a resonance between producers and consumers are created to go beyond economic value. Co-creating new functionality is the decisive factor for providing consumers with more benefits, including not only affordability but also convenience, comfort and identity.

This innovation success will be realized by three steps – observation, design and delivery. First, producers should build new forms of interaction with consumers. All producers must start with observation on the ground to define the need. Producers need to develop new skills and knowledge for a greater appreciation and a deeper understanding of social, cultural, aspirational and emotional needs. Second, new functionality will be developed through a resonance between producers and consumers. An ability to collaborate across boundaries is required to exchange thoughts and feelings for a better design of new functionality. Diverse perspectives to deal with complex issues are also necessary to combine ideas of individuals and resources of organizations for better innovation outcomes. Third, the realized new functionality will be delivered to consumers and be shared widely. Sharing new functionality does not mean adaptation. It should be reshaped to satisfy customers' own social, cultural, aspirational and emotional needs.

The purpose of work should be to co-create new functionality that meets broader societal expectations beyond economic value. Both producers and consumers need to work together in a co-evolutionary way to not only achieve economic success, but also respond to social, cultural, aspirational and emotional needs. These efforts will allow organizations to grow sustainably and individuals to improve their quality of life. Co-creating new functionality offers a chance to innovate work for a better future of the world.

Innovation Culture

How Does the British Snowman Work? The Disruptive Characteristic of British Snow

Keith Bevis and Mariana Dodourova

British snow is so different. In every other country, snow is either just the stuff of pictures or a real part of life; a regular intrusion that must be planned for, managed, a known obstacle, a tourist attraction, a sport. In Britain, however light the covering, snow is a disruptive event. It makes us do things in different ways; change our plans, travel different paths, meet different people.

Key to any understanding of work in the knowledge-based industries are skills, communications and travel. Although they allow us to innovate, are we in danger of categorizing and qualifying innovation to a standstill? Do we need a snowman to reshape our work patterns and tools and provide the next disruptive step?

Breaking up Fixed Patterns

The story of skills in the latter part of the twentieth century has been one of handing down expertise. The quality systems from Japan filtering down through tier upon tier of manufacturing, bringing greater uniformity to manufacturing industry. This has brought some fantastic achievements; greater precision, more control, less waste and so much more competitive pricing. But when we look at the snowflakes of small to medium-sized enterprises (SME's), we ask why with all these impressive techniques they are not developing and growing. Like snowflakes, they come into existence, perform, change, dissolve and vanish. Our snowman's first lesson is that however light the snowflakes are, they have the right characteristics to build into an impressive structure for just as long as it is needed.

In the knowledge based-industries almost all our innovation and output is embedded in communication. Rather like snow our ideas seem to be formed in the "Cloud". On the one hand our ideas become freer, more communicable, more open. But like the century before, there are controlling influences wanting to categorize in order to marshal, to control. Large corporations have embraced open innovation, promoting its successes and offering its promises to the smaller competition, just like the manufacturing skills previously. By contrast, small enterprises for the most part seem reluctant to step out and discover. They need a white landscape of snow where they can place a first foot, make a definite mark, be seen.

The regular routine of work travel that fits with our work timing provides part of the framework for our fixed daily patterns. Innovation requires us to think differently, to juxtapose ideas and accept the risk involved. Fixed patterns militate against looking for differences. When the snow falls we are shaken up. We struggle to find ways of achieving our work goals during the disrupted period. The disruption further challenges the stability of our working framework. It is precisely this level of disruption that we need as a stimulus for innovation. For that level of creative disruption to become part of our working environment we must challenge the notion of people continuing to work for one employer at one place!

From Open Innovation to Open Working

Occasional snowfall to make us think differently about how and where we work is not a reliable way to encourage and stimulate innovation. What the snow does tell us is that however efficient we have become, however much we have driven down costs and time to market, the casualty might just have been our ability throughout industry to spontaneously innovate.

Smart "Portfolio Man" has taught us that it is possible for the brightest to choose how they work and to do it in a personally fulfilling way. Snow teaches us that dramatic changes in working patterns can be for everyone. Snow starts as a constant all-embracing covering treating everyone the same. How we cope with snow in our lives is a very individual choice.

Open innovation is a paradigm embraced by companies with a strong understanding of intellectual property and the ability to attract new ideas and ways of thinking. Perhaps within smaller and some may say more conservative organizations, the time has come to embrace open working, free of permanence and stability. Instead of protecting old skills, the snow flurry of new eyes and new ideas has the potential to bring new opportunities into our enterprises. With new staff in our enterprise we could overcome barriers, travel in different ways to different places and so learn about other situations, problems and models of working. Can we accept the risk of having our staff float like snowflakes, not always being at the same job but drifting as the wind (work) demands?

Can we begin to understand that our internal organizational structures must respond to our individual company needs? Uniformity and convention no longer guarantee success in today's turbulent business environment: companies must embrace change and uncertainty, and continuously adapt to external pressures. This necessitates a wide range of connections within and outside organizations with the potential for unplanned connections. How do organizational units need to be created and defined to foster initiative, collaboration and flexibility, encompass different patterns of interaction and retain continuity? Open working requires unfreezing existing structures, processes, and routines, and opening people up to different possibilities to provoke creativity and invent new ways of seeing and doing things. Moreover, the need for adaptive integration and improved coordination across multiple capabilities highlights the necessity to link internal structures and activities more closely with networks of complementary structures and activities outside organizations. Like snowflakes piling together and reaching critical mass and quality, networks of small firms can simultaneously realize integration, flexibility, and innovation hence emulating the advantages of large corporations, but in a flexible and adaptive manner.

The concept of open working presupposes a buoyant market, but if it brings innovation and growth, it would indeed develop that type of market. The snowman would have us walking in the air.

A New Openness: How to Deal with New Challenges as Open Innovation and Crowdsourcing Become Standards in Management Practice

Birgit Fingerle, Anna Maria Köck and Klaus Tochtermann

Today limited to a small number of groundbreaking organizations, open innovation and crowdsourcing are two management approaches that we expect to become an integral part of management practice within the next decade. Allowing organizations to benefit from the collective intelligence of an external workforce, they have the potential to revolutionize the way we work. While open innovation is dedicated to opening up innovation processes to external stakeholders such as customers or a broad public, in order to integrate their know-how and creativity in innovation tasks, crowdsourcing is defined more broadly. It comprises outsourcing all kinds of tasks to an open or defined crowd via the web. This may include, for example, tasks related to data entry by volunteers or paid microworkers. In contrast, open innovation also comprises offline activities, like lead user workshops, in addition to online activities such as idea contests.

Nevertheless, these new collaboration models have a lot in common with regard to their impact on organizations and their employees. They allow organizations to benefit from the sought-after creativity, knowledge, qualifications or just free time of externals to accomplish their tasks. This can enrich business processes and lead to competitive advantages since the integration of external "lead users" is more likely to create products that are very innovative and offer high customer value. The associated risks are manifold, e.g. with regard to intellectual property issues, protection of business secrets or potential public relations challenges.

New Questions Arise

One fear is that these approaches will weaken the standing of employees. But neither will open innovation make innovation management or internal R & D redundant, nor will crowdsourcing set free most of the salaried workforce. Far from it! But it is also true that their implementation will probably not leave employees unscathed. To use these approaches properly will demand significant changes to organizational practices: Forming new models of cooperation with people outside the organization, opening up the organization and dealing with new, flexible organizational boundaries. New answers will be needed to the question of what an organization is and where it ends to fully use the potential of these approaches beyond the next decade.

At the innovation project level, crowdsourcing and open innovation will have become part of the "usual" set of tools in the future. An important basis for making innovation projects run efficiently is the seamless integration of virtual (web-based) tools and applications into the current work environment of the persons involved. Innovation or project managers will either have tested models and intelligent applications based on semantic technologies that help them decide when to use which tools, or they will be trained to evaluate and decide in each phase of the innovation process if it would be of use to integrate externals. This implies changes to existing job profiles and the arrival of new job profiles. 'Integration managers' will be needed that are able to assess and advise their colleagues on whether and how to open up a specific task. They will know how to design and manage open projects, motivate externals and engage in networking activities inside and outside the organization.

At the organizational level, more creativity and a 'new openness' will be required for the successful adaption of open innovation and crowdsourcing. Today, organizational cultures and individual professional roles lag behind the new possibilities, often dominated by the fear of being replaced by externals. A 'new openness' will be needed with regard to the perception of an organization and its environment, the division of labor, and the division of roles. It can lead to the definition of new core competencies and new business models.

From an individual's point of view, dealing with uncertainty, more complexity and flexibility, testing new organizational boundaries, cooperating with new partners in new ways can easily cause disorientation and confusion. Questions such as: Where do I belong? Whom can I trust? What information may I give to whom? will arise.

Implications for Work Design

This in turn raises an important question at the organizational level: How can an organization prevent the behavior of its employees from contradicting its external efforts? Answering this question appropriately will require a new definition of the employee's standing, as well as living a new openness in internal relations. We believe that the role of employees will become even more important when applying open innovation and crowdsourcing in a long-term and sustainable way. The more openness an organization chooses, the less it can afford to leave its employees alone, and the more it will have to focus on their appreciation and commitment. Most successful at dealing with the new challenges will be the organizations that follow the humanistic ideal of man and answer the one central question, over and over again: How can we best support our employees in dealing with this new openness?

These organizations will do everything they can to support their employees in being autonomously, creatively thinking and acting personalities. In such an environment, human resource development and organizational development will become even more important. Personality development will be at its center and will be fuelled by manifold measures, e.g. by organizing peer consulting groups for project team members, training internal coaches, or assigning external coaches. New tools for knowledge management or personal apps which foster creative thinking will facilitate this. Expecting entrepreneurial thinking, flexibility and creativity of its employees, an organization in return has to grant freedom and a protective, error-tolerant space. Why? Because confident employees with a strong professional identity will be able to reflect on their professional roles and different stakeholders' goals, and will master the questions connected to the new openness.

Creating Future Knowledge Work

Peter Brödner

"Innovation is creativity selected by competition" (*Horst Albach*) and competition is increasingly driven by innovations. Innovations creatively transform knowledge into business. They are, therefore, based on knowledge work, i.e. on work in processes of generating, organizing and suitably using knowledge in given situations. In this respect, the basic distinctions between implicit and explicit knowledge or between working capacity and codified knowledge about work are highly relevant.

Working capacity denotes the practical action competence of humans based on their experiences as well as on their reflective, operative and co-operative capabilities to effectively act in a situation in order to realize their own intentions and interests. Action competence proves itself in successful situated actions; it comprises the capacity to interpret situations as a whole as well as procedural routines to suitably act in them. Action competence grows with experience and by appropriating and effectively applying explicit knowledge.

Explicit or codified knowledge on the other hand denotes experiential knowledge brought into consciousness by reflection and concept formation: Human practice is structured and partially explicated by relevant concepts. Explicit knowledge takes the form of theories, i.e. systems of consistently related concepts and propositions about practice. Theories explain how things work (comprehension). They are self-referentially closed and need to be appropriated through action competence in order to effectively change a practice (problem solving).

Without human action competence or working capacity, innovations could not be produced and inevitably related uncertainties could not be coped with. Without action competence it would also be impossible to manage and to suitably and effectively apply the fast rising tides of differentiated codified knowledge for situated problem solving and innovations, to assess the relevance of knowledge, to enable co-operation and sharing of knowledge between experts of different domains, and to appropriate explicit knowledge for putting it to effective use.

Within knowledge work, subjective working capacity thus regains its relevance lost in the course of Tayloristic objectification of work by explicating knowledge about work processes and reification as machines ("*scientification*"). To the extent, however, to which explicit or codified production knowledge is creatively used during entrepreneurial competition for innovating products, services and processes, the diversity, complexity, dynamics, and uncertainties of related products, processes and markets increase while imposing growing requirements on human working capacity. Hence, the importance of and requirements for subjective action competence increase, while and because the abstract work force, as subject to processes of capital valorization, is increasingly being objectified in the form of codified knowledge and technical artifacts. Objectification of work thus turns into subjectification.

This epochal turnover comes hand in hand with *new forms of control*. Working capacity is bound to the bodily existence of the individuals owning it and as such it is unalienable (except by partial explication as knowledge). Working capacity can only unfold through self-determined work, knowledge sharing and co-operation with other individuals. In order to nonetheless realize capital valorization requirements in autonomous, self-organizing working teams, new forms of control are needed: *indirect contextual control* by market requirements instead of hierarchical command and control schemes (that cannot be practiced under uncertainty and without planning anyhow). Under permanent pressure to succeed, the individual workers owning the working capacity drive themselves towards the highest possible performance, albeit at the cost of their health and social relationships, always at the risk of undermining their working capacity through long-lasting excessive demands.

In fact, the number of stress disorders like sleep disturbances, burnout syndromes, depressions or drug abuse has increased epidemically over the last 15 years, in particular in the domains of highly qualified knowledge work. Almost a decade of own analytical and empirical research on multifunctional team work in IT development and consulting projects – as a typical area of knowledge work – point to the causes of these disorders. Based on the concept of *contradicting work demands*, a number of recurring mismatches between work requirements, actually available resources and effective rules were identified that can explain the observed disorders. Similar mismatches between performance pressure and actually available resources can frequently be observed, as a consequence of indirect control schemes, in many other areas of qualified knowledge work.

Remedy can, due to the complex nature of cause and effect relationships, only be achieved if improvements on several action layers – at the individual, organizational, and institutional levels – are implemented:

- Coping competences for stress are normally developed to different degrees among individuals; this means that they can be learned to a certain degree through coaching, for instance.
- At the level of work organization, systematic efforts can be made to avoid imbalances between work demands and actually available resources, e.g. by providing influence on work demands and effort estimation, by avoiding parallel project work or by following evolutionary project management procedures.
- At the institutional level, coping with uncertainty inherent in structural change requires higher levels of social security conducive to sustaining working capacity, e.g. by active labor market policies or new working time regulations allowing long-term balancing of time accounts.

These core challenges to developing a prosperous knowledge society still need strong efforts in research and exploration.

Thinking Outside the Box – How Companies Can Benefit from Cooperation with External Creatives

Celina Proch and Agata Siuda

Creative industries are taking a leading role in transforming Germany's economy into a knowledge-based one. The creative scene already uses future-oriented work and business models, such as hybrid working methods, and is highly innovative. Companies from the non-creative sector could overcome "tunnel vision" by opening their innovation processes to external input from creatives. This is a look at to what degree creative methods can be implemented in work processes and established as a systematic component of companies' added value for the work environments of the future, describing a possible application of this concept based on the pilot project *Creative Drive* initiated by the *GründerZentrum Kulturwirtschaft Aachen.*

Creative Input for Companies – a Case Study

A musician, a carpenter, two product designers, one industry designer, and a graphic designer are working together on a project to develop solutions for an IT-company. What might seem incongruous at first could turn into a winning concept in consulting: *Creative Drive* operates on the principle of uniting actors from the creative industries on teams developing solutions for companies – in this case, identifying new ways to boost the company's brand and product with emotion, and inspiring employees to become more innovative. The biggest advantage of such a cooperative project is the outside perspective that the external creatives bring to the table. The potential of interdisciplinary groups is the constructive approach to the creative process, something that differs in each artistic discipline. Everyone on the team is proficient in unique and specific techniques and strategies. These methods are then applied to an area outside of their specialties in order to facilitate an unbiased approach to the problem: Consequently, naiveté and lack of specialization are not a disadvantage but instead, result in a desired benefit, "This is the only way to break through habitual, cookie-cutter structures and leave the beaten path," says Kai Hennes (a musician and member of *Creative Drive*). Against this background, it is essential that the creatives keep working mainly in their own discipline, retaining their specific approaches.

Although the group has won a nationwide innovation award for their concept, in this case, the client did not implement the solution, deeming it too artistic. "Communication is the key," says Hennes, concluding that they should have communicated much earlier during the creative process in order to better match the visions and needs of the company.

Implications for Future Cooperation

For successful cooperation, both sides – the company as well as the creatives – need to compromise. Creatives have to be willing to focus their creative potential on an objective without relinquishing their creative freedom. They must also retain a certain amount of freshness and innovation without losing focus of what the client wants. Consequently, it is critical that the creatives practice their discipline of origin to retain their unique approach to problem solving. Additionally, training in marketing can support their ability to relate to the clients' concerns.

Companies in turn have to be willing to change habitual and unconscious patterns of action. On the one hand, they have to muster the courage to get involved with something completely new because that is the only way they can be considered innovative. On the other hand, they have to acknowledge their problems and weaknesses. Decision-makers have to take the time to precisely state their goals and to identify where exactly the problems lie. As communication is crucial for successful cooperation, the companies need to provide a contact who keeps in constant touch with the creatives. This facilitator should not only provide necessary information but also offer the creatives a chance for closer contact with the employees and supply them with more insight into the business and production. This would help sensitize the creatives for the clients' evolving needs. Offering work space in the company during the period of cooperation could be one possible way of supporting this experience. Finally, companies have to be willing to compensate the performance of the creatives adequately and provide a realistic schedule.

Successful cooperation would result in advantages for the companies as well as for the creatives involved: companies would be able to solve problems in different ways and learn a creative, free way of thinking, and creatives would learn from their experiences of working together on teams from different areas with their distinct approaches to addressing completely new challenges. This experience could prove very advantageous for their own work.

In the long run, the integration of creative professionals into business processes would result in an atmosphere of innovation throughout an entire corporation. With several participating businesses, this could steer corporate culture into a highly beneficial direction. Generating innovation will become more important in the future; this kind of cooperation will help reach this goal.

A first step into this future is making known that such cooperation between companies and creatives is possible. The next challenge will be creating the infrastructure that will offer matching and mediating services between companies and creatives. The Internet and forums where creatives can present their areas of specialization, and companies can describe their problems would help bring the two sides together. If the structural parameters can be established, the future could be marked by an increase in successful cooperation, and many industries could profit from creative input.

The Celebrity in Your Firm – Your Firm as a Celebrity

Martin Kamprath

The Rise of Symbolic Value Creation for Innovation

Over the past years, the importance of the creative industries as a main pillar of economic development has increased enormously. The creative industries function as a catalyst, directly or indirectly stimulating the innovation system regarding the diffusion of new technologies in the wider economy. Additionally, the dogmatic role of technology as the one and only driver of innovation is questionable and needs to be revisited, considering the success of Apple, Samsung, Google, Facebook and other design-driven companies. These kinds of companies do not primarily base their innovation success on technological development. Instead, they offer new product/service systems that do not only add functional value for the customers, but also emotional meaning or cultural symbols. If we consider consumption as a part of a social practice, buyers of Apple products do not only own a device for making calls and surfing the Internet. They also express their affirmation of a certain social group and a certain lifestyle. The creation of such emotional realities is seen as one of the core activities of companies within the creative industries. The increasing relevance of symbolic value creation will form the basis of such a future vision for the aspects of and within companies that create products that are not only technologically innovative. Given the importance of symbolic value creation, the concept of "(Corporate) Celebrities" adds an interesting perspective to the vision of the future, suggesting a different understanding of the role of companies and especially, of the role of their employees.

Celebrities as Anchors for Innovation Attention

Celebrities are people who have gained an enormous reputation through public attention. Celebrities show talent, lots of energy and "drive." They are often "winners," have a strong presence in the media and are famous "because they are famous." Sometimes their talent is not rooted in unique capabilities, but in their personality or lifestyle, which is shaped by them. Celebrities are symbols or icons that present a certain way of living, they are someone to admire or detest for what and how they act and see the world. In other words, celebrities gain public attention because their appearance generates emotional resonance.

In the creative industries, celebrities are not only found in front of the camera. The star-system also works in the background. Star architects, fashion designers, film directors or bestselling authors attract attention with their name in industries where success is quite unpredictable and often short-term. The implicit knowledge of creative work and the extremely important reputation and status of single persons are often the only indicators by which to estimate a project outcome (the "nobody knows anything" paradigm). Due to an increase in media reporting, new forms of corporate communication, and changes in media consumption, the celebrity concept now also applies to the corporate level. Some companies attract media attention like celebrities. Companies in the media, ICT or web sectors receive icon status because they shape the lifestyle of millions of people. One can predict an increase in this trend in the future. While in the past, movie and sports celebrities were used to build a corporate brand through advertising, in the world of tomorrow, the celebrity status of the firm itself as well as of some employees will become a driver of innovation diffusion. If single positions no longer carry a certain job description, but depend on skill sets instead, if social networks and the internet make it ever easier to find information about individuals, if it becomes more and more apparent who stands behind a corporate brand, and if the imprinting of symbols and lifestyles is seen as a part of innovation, then single individuals from different company levels shift into focus. This personification opens the previously black boxes of a company to outsiders. Extraordinary persons could become a brand of their own, thus receiving the status of (corporate) celebrities. Companies will pay attention to these individuals because they satisfy the media hunger for highlighted extremes and communicable stories to create emotions and immersion. This way, the corporate reputation and brand will enter into symbiosis with the celebrities working for the company. Celebrity and company may fuse in the consumer's mind.

Celebrities Can Act as a Catalyst for the Implementation or Diffusion of Radical Innovations

Dealing with celebrity status will generate a different consciousness within companies as to how to handle public attention and celebrity status. Generally, it will affect the balance between (technical) innovation activities and the conditions for diffusion. For the latter, the advantage of celebrity status is that society will not sanction unconventional behavior negatively, because to some degree, celebrities stand above these norms. Therefore, celebrities can act as a catalyst for the implementation or diffusion of radical innovations. On the one hand, celebrity status is an intangible and highly volatile resource. Celebrities as persons can hardly be retained for long by a company, because they are restless and try to improve their situation. They will search for new projects or tasks that suit or broaden their brand and reputation. On the other hand, celebrities will act as a magnet for new talents. For example, in the creative industries and other areas characterized by individual skills and uncertainty about project outcomes, some employees still work at low rates, or even for free. Working together with celebrities such as star architects or movie directors is seen as part of the payment in terms of reputation, allowing better standing for future projects or positions. Although celebrities may be fluctuating and therefore risky assets, they provoke emotional involvement for customers and employees. They are lighthouses and reference points in a complex and multifaceted world.

How to Build Organizational Trust in an Unpredictable and Turbulent Environment

Kirsimarja Blomqvist

This article critically examines traditional sources of organizational trust are and discusses means for building trust in unpredictable and uncertain environments. Both academics and practitioners view trust as a valuable, higher-order resource that supports organizing. Basically trust has been seen as a threshold condition in efficient communication and collaboration. Trust makes it possible to rely on others, disclose valuable information and combine specialized and dispersed knowledge. In contemporary organizations trust can be seen to be a critical resource allowing individuals to take actions and accomplish their tasks efficiently and effectively. However, the levels of trust in organizations have been decreasing due to the global socio-economic crisis and subsequent layoffs, virtual and temporary structures, as well as continuous technological and organizational changes. The so-called psychological contract of mutual expectations between committed employees and organizations providing long-term employment has been broken and many employees are no longer able and willing to trust large organizations.

Building and sustaining organizational trust is by no means easy. Supervisor communication and behavior are always critical sources for interpersonal organizational trust. Organizational processes, structures as well as top management behavior build impersonal organizational trust. Interpersonal and impersonal organizational trust are seen to complement each other and together they can provide stronger trust. What follows is a discussion of means to support organizational trust in unpredictable and uncertain environments.

Predictability

In the past bureaucratic organizations operating in a stable environment could build trust based on *predictability*. In a dynamic environment this is basically no longer possible due to continuous organizational, technological and socio-political changes. However, there are some sources for predictability that organizations can build and rely on. For example, an inclusive strategy process, transparent organizational decision-making and HRM processes can provide some predictability and can thus function as sources for impersonal organizational trust. They can be especially important in situations where inter-personal trusting ties are thin and fragile, e.g. when supervisors change, work remotely or can only commit less effort and face-to-face time for leadership activities.

Identification

Organizations striving for strategic and operational flexibility organize work increasingly through temporary workers and external partners, leading to a situation where employees lack a shared history or social similarity. Organizations also try to use dispersed knowledge and competences efficiently across organizational borders by building competence centers that provide experts for various temporary projects. In modern organizations *identification*, a traditional source for organizational trust, can no longer be based on a shared past, social similarity or proximity. This type of identification could even be detrimental to organizations trying to leverage dispersed knowledge effectively. Instead, organizations can try to build identification based on a shared vision and shared future, if they are able to build an inclusive culture and inspiring future in which employees can participate.

Supporting and rewarding capability

Capability-based trust provides a strong basis for organizational trust. If employees know that the organization has a fair and solid recruitment process and only capable individuals are recruited and rewarded, this provides a strong basis for organizational trust. In turbulent times, it is not only continuous learning but also organizational unlearning that must be proactively supported when capabilities and skills are not sufficient or become even detrimental for contemporary environmental requirements. For example nepotism and use of closed social capital is not acceptable in today's business environment, which requires the use of the best talent and ideas as well as high ethical values.

Positive intentions

Positive intentions build organizational trust if top management and supervisors invest in communicating openly about their values, motives and goals. This requires honesty and good communication skills. If top management is considered as authentic and truly aiming for positive organizational goals, even difficult decisions such as cost cutting or laying off employees can be accepted more easily. It is in such difficult decisions that fairness and transparency of the decision-making process especially support employee trust.

Positive affect

The willingness and ability to see continuous change as an opportunity instead of a risk require an organizational climate with positive affect. Work tasks requiring creativity and problem solving in teams also require affect-based trust for employees to be willing to share personal and tacit knowledge. A climate of positive affect can be supported by thoughtful behavior, such as greetings, saying thank you and celebrating small everyday positive outcomes, e.g. when finishing a project in time, and showing public appreciation for employees who have helped others, invested in learning or engaged in organizational citizenship behavior. In addition mindfulness, respect, and even humor can create positive affect that supports trust.

Implications for Work Design

It has been argued that different work tasks require trust in different ways. The more complex and tacit the knowledge, and the more interdependent the employees, the higher the need for trust. Increasingly highly complex and ambiguous work tasks carried out in teams of specialized experts require strong trust built by complementary means, e.g. supporting capability-, identification-, and affect-based organizational trust. Further, the higher the speed of change, the more important the roles of identification and intention in communicating the shared vision of supporting employee trust and commitment. As one of the very successful leaders puts it: if you can build a shared vision, you can run the extra mile!

Virtual Work

Virtual Work 3.0: Beyond Today's Social Media

Eilif Trondsen

Because of exponential technological change we will see much more effective ways of doing and managing globally distributed work by 2020. These changes may extend far beyond the current "2D Web trajectory." The next 3–4 years will see growing competition between "apps and the Web" or between the "closed, controlled and highly integrated" ecosystem led by Apple and the more open ecosystem of choice led by Google and its growing number of partners. But another development that has not yet appeared on the radar screen of most observers of today's technology landscape is the emergence of browser-based, 3D immersive environments (or IEs, for short, which Google is contributing to bringing about through its Chrome browser that will integrate WebGL and take advantage of HTML5 and other technologies that are emerging).

What advantages will these developments bring us? And what are their implications for how work can and will be done? The answers depend in part on how fast emerging technology will address two overarching weaknesses of today's IEs: Cumbersome access (needing to first download a "heavy client" and then needing to learn to use the interface for creating one's avatar, or one's digital representation) and then learning what for most users is non-intuitive navigation of the 3D environment. These weaknesses – and there are also others – explain at least to some degree why IEs have not seen the rapid adoption that many analysts expected around the mid-2000s.

Virtual Work in 2020

Here is a possible scenario for what kind of a virtual work environment we may have in 2020:

I am an independent contractor with an office in a nice bungalow located on a Pacific island – all virtual in an IE. I paid a few hundred dollars to a 3D builder, who built my house using a free and open source platform and tools. The island is owned and managed by an entrepreneur who has set up virtual houses and offices, providing a variety of business services to residents.

When I work on projects, I send a meeting invitation including a URL that the team members click on and immediately get teleported into my very nice and luxurious virtual conference room, where we all are represented by our avatars. The other project team members all were able to quickly create their own avatars and no one had to learn how to navigate the environment as they now use a gestural interface that the new IE had created by leveraging Microsoft's Kinect technology introduced in the fall of 2010. The face of my avatar also now reflects my emotions when I interact with the other virtual team members, so they recognize various non-verbal cues as part of our communication during our meetings.

In my impressive conference room I also have a number of other tools that allow more effective collaborative work than before with team members anywhere in the world. These tools include:

- Virtual video conferencing system;
- Interactive and live sharing whiteboards for brainstorming sessions;

– Interactive Google docs that can be displayed on large screens.

One of our recent projects required the prototyping of a new and revolutionary part for a new nano-scale robotic device. Our Korean designer and Norwegian engineer both teleported into the meeting and we created a 3D model of the device at a scale 10,000 times bigger than the actual part for the device. This allowed us to enter the interior of the part and examine its complex circuitry, to make sure it had the right specs.

At very low cost, I feel I have a great and very functional (virtual) "home office" – and with facilities and surroundings that I could not replicate in real life – and as a result, work has now become a much more enjoyable experience.

A work environment like the one in the scenario above will bring new opportunities for both individuals and enterprises. The IE will allow building trust with distributed collaborators from anywhere in the world, and enabling quick formation of highly diverse global teams, accessing talent from anywhere.

Large enterprises can also gain significant advantages. In 2010, BP used IEs to train cross-functional teams in leadership skills, and many other companies explored various applications of IEs around the same time. In 2020 all of these large companies see cost-effective use of IEs in their daily operations.

No opportunity comes without potential risks. Employees would experience frustration, waste of time and cost if enterprises do not design and implement IEs appropriately. Excessive dependence on virtual technologies is also a potential risk, reducing employees' ability to handle traditional environments well.

Implications for Work Design

The emergence of IEs that are much easier to access and use than today's technology platforms will give individuals and enterprises new options. Here are a few implications for work design:

- Greater freedom and options for globalizing work teams and staffing these teams;
- More global, synchronous work will bring challenges due to time-zone differences;
- Work and social interaction and leisure – if all virtual – can be integrated more than before;
- Increasing work satisfaction if properly organized and managed.

My Workplace Will Be Mobile – And Is Already

Uwe Hauck

Thinking of the way I want to work in the future and looking at my tools and workplace today leads me to the conclusion that finally we have reached a point where there are no more technological obstacles to working wherever and whenever we want. Two key technologies are the foundation for making the switch to a working environment focused on results rather than presence in a specific physical place. First with both broadband mobile access and broadband at home and in the workplace, services can be delivered wherever we are. Second, mobile device are becoming more and more powerful so we can perform all necessary tasks while on the road.

Coordinating Life in the Cloud

To me, the cloud, which is nothing more than another metaphoric naming for the internet finally allows us to use it as both our source of information as well as our global storage system. I myself am a heavy user of Google's service infrastructure. Starting with Google Docs, communicating via Google Chat and Google Hangouts using Google Calendar and Google Mail I coordinate both my personal as well as my professional life in the cloud.

This has two main advantages. First, there is no need to manually sync any device when at my PC. All data are in the cloud, being served to my device constantly. And by allowing selected colleagues access to certain documents I can work with partners on document drafts or create new ideas, new concepts in a sort of online brainstorming process

My personal infrastructure regarding hardware consists of only three devices. First, the smartphone is my basic communication platform for traditional voice calls as well as messaging. But for me messenger services like Google Chat or MSN have already eliminated the need to use test messages Second and mostly for its convenience I use a tablet for browsing the web, blogging while on the road and not willing to "unpack" all my stuff It gives me the freedom to do my writing, do my research and yes, it is also my preferred format for entertainment while on the road.

Last but not least, there is my notebook, which also replaces the need for a desktop computer at home. While on the road it is my full blown blogging and working platform playing my presentations, allowing me to work as if I were at the office. At home, with the addition of a big flat screen monitor, a keyboard and a mouse it transforms into my desktop PC with all the convenience you could ever expect.

Integrated Work Platforms of the Future

But yet, we are talking about several devices. This leads me to the following vision for a future environment. I expect these rather diverse platforms to become combined into one or as a maximum two platforms for all of our work. We will see the tablet, notebook and ultrabook form factor combined into one device in the future. This device will allow us to work with the display as if it were a tablet, but also use it as the monitor for the ultra/notebook that it also represents.

And it will come with all the services from the cloud already installed. I envision the discussion regarding the right operating system becoming obsolete sooner or later. As more and more of our tools and apps and yes, also games are heading for the cloud, we no longer really care which operating system gives us access to our personal cloud. Maybe in future we will even work with only one device, something like a superphone of which the currently available Samsung Galaxy Note gives us merely a glimpse. This new phone will be able to dock to whatever display front end we want.

With this future environment comes a discussion about social impacts and data security. So we will have to discuss some aspects of this future environment. First of all, its social impact, which will play a major role in Marc Paczian's article regarding the social impacts of the new ways of mobile and flexible work. Second we need to reconsider such aspects as data security as we will share more documents on the net, and collaborate on them with tools of the social media kind.

I am not sure if we already have the right tools for new ways of collaboration as there is always the mix of private and public, of confidential and open. Maybe we need a second infrastructure for our companies, based on the technologies we already know and use but working in a private cloud. These new infrastructures will be served by our employer's IT departments yet allow us to access them from anywhere in the cloud. We need to recognize the mix we will experience, the boundaries between private/personal use of IT and infrastructures and public use and implement strategies to keep the confidential data secure from public access–and all this without imposing two separate networks.

Virtualization of Work

When thinking of virtualization I believe we will experience more and more virtual work environments closed to public access and under the security control of the IT-department, which will allow access to sensitive business data by separating them from the real operating system of our mobile device as a means of restricting access. It will be as if we use two computers, one for the sensitive data and one for everyday chat and work on the web. There might be dedicated access points for exchanging data, but in the most secure environments the mobile device will merely be a display for the data processed securely on the servers of the IT departments.

And to conclude my excursion in the future of mobile work: I do myself practice most of what I preach. I am already a heavy user of cloud services and work on several operating systems without really "feeling" the difference. And at least to me all those technologies have made work easier, more independent and more secure so that all I need is always also available on my "big bold net computer called the Internet"

But as I mentioned earlier: As we change the technological way we work we should not ignore the issue of social impact. The challenge today is not about the technologies at hand. The challenge is whether we as a society can implement new rules regarding future workplaces.

We Are Changing – How about Work?

Marc Paczian

As Uwe Hauck mentioned in his contribution from a technology perspective all the tools needed to enable the new ways of working, the workplace of the future, are already available. What I do see on the other hand is that from a cultural point of view there is still a long road ahead of us to reach the same maturity level.

Two Central Trends

The status quo is changing and it is changing rapidly. Current studies show that there are two trends that directly influence the ways of working. First of all the time when people are working is changing towards later (after 6 PM) and weekends. As the overall working hours didn't increase accordingly, this leads me to the conclusion that more and more people need flexible working time models. We do see that it is the output that matters, not the time it took you to generate it.

The second trend is an increase in people working in "higher qualified" jobs, e.g. knowledge workers. Their expectation towards collaboration, working methods and technology has already changed a lot and will be even more diverse and engaging in the future. So far, I cannot see this change happening in many companies. More than 50% of large corporations ban the use of external social networks, and they still they do not offer adequate internal alternatives.

Those two trends will continue to grow, with an explicit impact on work itself. Today's economy is more and more driven by innovation and change – both of them extremely fast. We need to get new products out on the market more and more quickly, at least faster than the competition. What we need to look at is: what kind of work environment do we need to achieve the best possible results?

One thing is very clear: you cannot flip on innovation and change with a little button inside your head. If you try to force employees to be creative you will fail. If you try to force employees to change you will fail. You will either get bad results or, even worse, loose the employee to your competition. What really motivates people is having the freedom to make their own decisions. The worst demotivation on the other hand is control. If you give employees the freedom to be creative, they will be creative. If you start to explain why change is necessary, they will change.

In the future companies, especially large enterprises, need to consider the needs and wishes of their employees much more than today. To do this, they first of all need to know what those needs and wishes are. I would like to highlight two very concrete things I come across very often.

When Do We Want to Work?

When I look at myself, I can distinguish less and less whether what I am currently doing is work or leisure. I frequently check what is new on Twitter, where I do follow some of my friends, but also colleagues, customers and competitors. I often also do this in the evening and on the weekend. Is that work or leisure? All employees in Germany can be forced to document their working hours and many companies expect them to do so. How can you document your working hours if you cannot decide whether what you are currently doing is work or leisure?

There are some reasons why it might make sense to document your working time, e.g. for self-control before suffering burnout. I believe though that if what you are doing is satisfactory and self-determined you will recognize this point before it is too late.

In the future companies will need to find ways to allow their employees to work when and how they want to work. It will no longer be a matter of physical presence but rather of excellent output. The place of work will no longer matter – whether you are inside a company building, at home or on the beach. If an employee has a good idea or solution for a project, it just does not matter if that happens at 11 PM, sitting in front of his beach house in Sweden.

People Hate to Change – Why Are So Many Forced to Do So?

Looking at the rising number of smartphones all around the world I tend to ask myself how many of these were directly bought by companies to be given to their employees. Only in the last quarter of 2011, Apple sold 15 million iPads, most of them probably for private use. People love their smartphones and tablets!

In the future companies will have to adopt the use of private or business smartphones and tablets and allow their employees to use them at work. In addition to all the enterprise apps that are already deployed (e.g. ERP, ECM, CRM) we will see a huge rise in enterprise apps being developed. I strongly believe that companies who do not support the mobility trend will have issues with getting innovative, creative and passionate employees on board.

Facebook has more than 800 million users, with 250 million photos being uploaded every day. The English version of Wikipedia has approx. 4 million articles with more than 7.5 billion page views every month. People love to share their knowledge!

There is no need any more to encourage employees to share their knowledge – they are already doing it. Yes, it is on a private basis, but why is that? Because many companies do not see the need yet to give employees the same tools within their company environment that they are already used to in private life. In the future companies that ban social media tools or/and don't provide adequate tools internally will see a huge lack in knowledge sharing and, again, problems with getting the most talented people.

We can already see a cultural change within our work environment in terms of flexibility, mobility and sharing. This trend will continue and even grow exponentially over the next years. The most successful companies of the future will have given their employees the freedom to choose when and how to work. And in return they will get the most motivated and talented people.

Virtual Teamwork – Panoptic or Interactive Work Design

Lauge Baungaard Rasmussen

The emergence of virtual teamwork represents a dynamic response to globalization, the growth of communication technologies and dismantling of industrial based organizational hierarchies. These developments pose new challenges as the completion of the distributed tasks must be integrated across the barriers of cultural differences, and with fewer face-to-face clues. Virtual teamwork involves special demands regarding communication, trust and knowledge. The implications for future work design are immense, and still open for clarification and discussion.

Key Factors of Virtual Teamwork

Virtual teamwork is defined as geographically dispersed entities depending on electronic communication for carrying out their work activities. Much of the time, the members of virtual teams will communicate asynchronously as they are working in different time zones. The reason is that different parts of the team may be in action throughout the full 24 hours of the day. Relying on flexible temporality as a differential factor ensured by increasingly powerful and mobile information-processing systems, virtual teamwork can enhance the options for searching for the lowest price and/or the best quality of work. Some of this knowledge may be coded in the machines, but another part is tacit. For instance, rhythm, pulse and tempo of bodily gestures are parts of creative face-to-face teamwork, but in virtual work relationships, they are visible only to a very limited degree. Managers can no longer 'shop up' as a means to ensure efficiency and quality of work. Direct supervision must be substituted by formalized performance measurement and/or trust. Trust may reduce the number of control procedures, but it may also increase opportunistic behavior including violation of contracts and/or relational norms, for instance by intentionally transmitting incorrect information or withholding relevant knowledge. This is not a new risk, but it has increased in virtual work relationships due to a number of cultural, social and technical factors.

The successful outcome of virtual team work depends on how well the members are able and willing to share and create knowledge across disciplinary, spatial and/or cultural boundaries, either asynchronously or in real-time communication. The capabilities to access a 'noise-free', unrestricted and transparent flow between creating, sharing, practicing and accumulating knowledge emerge as critical factors, but are apparently difficult to accomplish in virtual teamwork. The relative impacts of trust and distrust depend on the design and implementation of job descriptions and performance measurement, as well as on positive and negative incentives for behaving in an appropriate manner. When job descriptions are restricted to repetitive actions for some parts of the virtual team, and other parts are supposed to take care of the creative thinking, the relative dominance of distrust may be stronger than the trust between the two parts. When performance measurement serves as panoptic surveillance only, knowledge withholding is more likely to occur than knowledge sharing. The individual ability and motivation to collaborate effectively in virtual teamwork depend on a number of factors such as, for instance, individual and social values and norms, incentives, mutual feelings of responsibility and acceptance, a meaningful framework within which work can be carried out, and requisite variety of tasks. These factors must be taken into consideration in the design process of virtual work teams.

Implications for Work Design

- *Panoptic surveillance should be substituted by interactive team-based key performance indicators:* The idea of Bentham's 'Panopticon' is top-down surveillance (the 'gaze'). More and more sophisticated ICT systems have made it possible to record all individual acts to be observed in real-time or stored for later use. These systems undermine trust and restrict potential creativity in daily work, while precisely the opposite is needed in most virtual teamwork. Therefore, panoptic surveillance systems of individuals should be replaced by interactive, team-based performance measurement systems, including a few integrated but transparent indicators that are understandable and observable by all members of the team.
- *Assessment of team performance indicators should be used as input to learning:* Therefore, members of virtual teams should be involved together with system experts in order to ensure the appropriateness of the indicators. The results could then be used as input for workshops between the geographically dispersed team members, sometimes face-to-face and sometimes mediated through visual telecommunication. These workshops can enhance both knowledge-based trust and learning by using one or several interactive workshop methods.
- *Options for 'thinking out of the box' should be a part of all job descriptions and positively evaluated in performance measurement:* Knowledge consists of notions connected into associative networks. Creative acts should not only be restricted to particularly arranged workshops, but expected as part of the daily practice in virtual teamwork. In order to enhance daily creativity, openness towards feedback and new ideas as well as cross-boundary and multi-disciplinary knowledge-sharing should be integrated as core values in the organizational culture. A knowledge repository for storing and updating feedback and ideas achieved during actual onsite work will also sustain daily creativity, in particular when access is open and interactively designed.

How the Work Floor Could Be Managing the Grand Scheme: Gaming Simulation as Participatory Management

Sebastiaan Meijer

In the increasingly complex world of globalizing production and intertwined technical production systems, it is beyond doubt that all personnel, from strategic apex to operational core, needs to be aligned with and aware of the situation the company and its operations are in. Managers apply knowledge management, key personnel retention, team development, validation sessions and other concepts to about any major organization to manage the tacit knowledge and skill base required. What strikes me is that most of these concepts are driven top-down. It is the management that organizes the management of knowledge, it is rarely the work floor that can decide who is key personnel, and team development is usually the choice of a manager confronted with a non-functioning department. I believe that recent insights on gaming simulation can contribute here. Integrating gaming simulation in the daily work place of operators can empower them and make a significant contribution towards integrating knowledge throughout the organization.

Gaming Simulation by the Work Floor

Since 2008, I have been working with my team on the introduction of gaming simulation in the railway sector as a means to reduce the uncertainty in decision-making on innovations. Gaming simulation (or serious gaming) is usually applied to training and teaching situations; however, in our line of work we use it as a method to test possible designs for operational innovations. Sessions feature real operators in their own roles, which is what has led to new insights. Historically, rail operators, like train traffic controllers, have a bad reputation amongst management for their unwillingness to change their work flow and for their bad collaboration with innovations. The railway management companies that we work with each have their own ways of dealing with this, and all try to involve the operators in design discussions, etc. And yet, a huge gap between design and implementation of innovations still exists. Management accuses operators of not (being able or willing) to say their real opinion during meetings, and operators accuse management of not understanding their work.

Since the introduction of gaming simulation, we have observed a trend. During the gaming sessions, the operators show a heavily involved attitude and are willing to discuss every detail related to the topic. When the operators are put into their own roles in the simulation, they are suddenly able to discuss the pros and cons of the innovations to an extent never seen before in the organizations. The first results from implementations of innovations that used gaming during the design phase are coming in now, and there are strong indications that using this methods leads to better innovations and easier implementations.

Now, what would the next step be if you think along the line from discussion to management-organized gaming simulations? Given the heavy involvement of the operators, we are now starting to experiment with permanent gaming simulation tools on the work floor. We are building simulated versions of the work places and connect these to computer simulations of the operational process. In November 2011, we put the first version into the train traffic control center in Amsterdam and asked the operators to play one hour a day. We experienced mainly enthusiasm, and lots of experimentation from the operators in ways they would not be able to do in the live train flow. Work has to be done to make the simulations better, but then again, the operators were able to tell us clearly what needs to improve and where to make it a valuable tool for them to experiment with ideas that could make their operations better.

Implications for Work Design

The experiences described above make me wonder about the potential value of gaming simulation in a detailed, high-fidelity form in operations. Operators who were believed to be unwilling to change suddenly wanted to experiment. I pose two thoughts that have implications for work design. First, I think that the more operational work is bound to strict adherence to rules and procedures, the more operators will need a simulated reality next to it to play with. Second, I believe that experimentation in a simulated gaming reality will lead to more knowledge sharing with co-workers and management. For both statements we have seen first proofs, but as always with science: we will need much more research to actually prove them.

Musability

Stephen Downes

This morning I read a short item from *Mashable* describing some predictions being made for the next five years by IBM. Among more workaday predictions we've heard elsewhere – that biometrics will become mainstream, for example, or that mobile computing will end the digital divide – is a prediction that demands more attention: that mind reading will become a practical technology.

This seems more the stuff of science fiction than it does a practical reflection on the future of work. However, the technology itself is not science fiction. The technology already exists to allow a person to control the movement of a cube on the screen through the exercise of thought alone. As we design input devices of greater and greater sensitivity, phenomena that once appeared to us to be only mental – our thoughts and dreams, for example – will begin to appear as physical manifestations.

Musing ('mental using') will become commonplace. Musability will become an important science, as these interfaces will need to be able to support action without distracting us – if you think it's dangerous to drive while talking on a mobile phone, imagine how dangerous it will be to drive while interfacing with a poorly designed muser agent.

Most likely we will first experience these interfaces as games. We will play at rotating the cube or dropping the objects into the correct containers all the while adapting to new skills our children (or *their* children) will take for granted. These mental environments will become as real to us – and as important a part of our everyday lives – as places like Facebook and Twitter and World of Warcraft are today. It will, indeed, be difficult to imagine what the world was like before people were connected mentally.

It is tempting at first to see such devices as replacing our current control panels and input screens. And there is an advantage to be found in mental control of physical devices. For example, we can – with training – speed our reaction times. Or we can, through visualization, execute movements that might be difficult physically, such as balancing an object or reproducing an image. Mental controls also reduce the distraction physical movements create while driving or executing some other motor operation.

Musing, however, has the potential to have a much wider impact. The possibility of subsonic broadcast through, say, a tiny transmitter implanted in our ears, or through optical displays embedded in a contact lens, enables two-way communication. A person could interact with another person or device in an entirely inconspicuous manner. The clerk at the counter who smiles and welcomes you by name may be communicating with a complex computer program that tells her everything she needs to know in the time it takes the two of you to shake hands.

Or you may be communicating with each other subvocally. When you walk up to the counter your request has been prepared by your own computer system and is transmitted to her with a thought. She receives a short mental message acknowledging receipt and nods to you in response, while subsonically expressing her thanks for your patronage. Meanwhile your status – and your thoughts – is relayed instantly to other members of your workgroup, who receive them as updates as they participate in meetings or tasks of their own.

It seems like a small thing, internal communication instead of external. But as our machines become more able to respond to our thoughts, these communications will enable complex tasks to be performed by teams of people working in concert. Highly sensitive operations, like computer chip design or brain surgery, for example, will be performed entirely by thought, by operators working in fully immersive environments imagining their way through an environment. Close your eyes and picture yourself attaching neurons to each other – that's what it will feel like to you as nanobots perform the actual physical labor.

While it is tempting to linger on the practical and technical aspects of musability, these will seem superficial when considered against the social changes wrought by such intimate communications. It may be hard to imagine today technologies such as email and texting to be slow and cumbersome, but that is how it will feel to a muser. And the immediacy of such communications will change the way we relate to each other. Social organizations will become much more personal, and the idea that "it's just business" will be relegated to an age when you didn't know – or could pretend you didn't know – how people would *feel* when you worked with them.

Practical musing technology may still be five years away, and the rise of what the new version of *Wired* will call "Muser Nation" may be a generation to come, but just as we can see how network technologies have had a profound impact on today's social organizations, weakening the dominance of hierarchies and resulting in the rise of asymmetrical warfare, people power and crowdsourcing, so also the mentally connected society will experience a fundamental change. It is hopeful – but maybe not unrealistic – to talk of moving beyond merely communicating to an ethos of *caring*.

Two factors would bring such a future into being. First, we would need a science that allowed us to share not just vocalized thoughts but also our experiences, emotions and feelings. Such a science would be *technically* possible; the major question is rather whether it would be socially *acceptable*. And second, a mechanization of work such that the bulk of physical labor were performed mentally, through musable interfaces. In such a case, the practice of 'work' as we know it today becomes less like labor and more like art. In such an environment, we would work in order to become *engaged*, and the level of engagement becomes directly proportional to the emotional fulfillment we receive.

It is perhaps difficult today to imagine a society in which we work for something other than the bread on our table and the roof over our heads, but a combination of abundance energy and mental computation make a reorganization of the underlying economics a necessity. The less demand there is in society for physical labor, the more unfair and less efficient a distribution of wealth based on labor will become. And so as we transition into a post-wealth society, and as public access to the necessities of life become commonplace, new currencies of community and well-being will become paramount.

Workplace Innovation

Workplace Innovation for Better Jobs and Performance – The Most Important Developments in Modern Working Environments

Jürgen Howaldt, Ralf Kopp and Frank Pot

The capability to generate sustainable innovations under conditions of knowledge intensity is an eminent societal challenge, demanding more attention on the organizational level for a) *social innovations* and b) *new perceptions of how to generate innovations*. This requires the creation of modern work environments based on c) *workplace innovation* enabling more self-organization and allowing more freedom for individual formatting of job handling.

a) *Social innovations* become more important for finding sustainable solutions that meet a variety of societal needs (economical, ecological, social). Social innovation focuses on the change of patterns in social systems (e.g., organizations) referring to routines and rules of communication, interaction and coordination of actions. Social innovations may take place on the level of processes and operations (e.g., the process of generating innovations) or on the level of products and services. To understand this new (social) "nature of innovation" *(OECD)* as a driver of innovation and to see technology (only) as an enabler means to reverse traditional views of their relationship. The generation and diffusion of social innovations differ extremely from those of technological innovation.

b) Usually, sustainable innovations are not generated by single charismatic brains, brilliant thinkers or lonely entrepreneurs but rather the result of collaboration and interaction in widespread networks of different actors and knowledge workers as well as the result of intense communication with clients, users and consumers. This type of *open innovation* contains more than only internet-based approaches (even if they are supported by technologies like Web 2.0) and represents a *new paradigm of innovation*.

c) *Workplace innovation* could be seen as the implementation of social innovations at the level of the organization. It is defined as the implementation of new and combined interventions in the field of work organization, human resource management and supportive technologies. Workplace innovation is considered to be complementary to technological innovation. Workplace innovation represents a *big shift* towards more participation, more decentralization of responsibility, more job autonomy, higher internal and external control capacity, more self-organization and learning opportunities, as well as the fostering of organizational and individual absorptivity of and connectivity to external knowledge and expertise. Workplace innovation also includes the ergonomic design of workplaces and an adequate IT infrastructure. We identified the most advanced approaches in so-called *enterprises 2.0.* High involvement and commitment is combined with high performance and innovativeness. Mature enterprises 2.0 could be defined as *socio-digital innovation systems*.

What Are the Opportunities and Risks for Future Working Life?

Introducing workplace innovation allows the improvement of quality of working life (QWL), well-being and the development of talents, and at the same time, the improvement of organizational performance. Workplace innovation aims at win-win situations, combining social and economic goals. Other concepts (e.g. sustainable work systems, high involvement workplaces, innovative workplaces, and new world of work) cover more or less the same topics. Research shows that simultaneous improvement of organizational performance and quality of working life is possible if those objectives are purposefully combined and if the employees and their supervisors are involved.

However, a lot of managers are not equipped for participatory approaches and/or are afraid to share power with their employees. Trust is a difficult asset to develop. Furthermore, defensive routines are hard to overcome, as they have been successful for a long time. Several hundred years ago, management was *invented* (and improved in the following centuries) to coordinate the emerging industrial work. It is not yet widespread knowledge that the organization and leadership of knowledge-intensive workplaces and knowledge workers demands a fundamental renewal of the basics of interaction and collaboration.

The diffusion of workplace innovation does not only need more promotion. It can lead to new profiles of risks and psychosocial constraints as well as the exclusion of older and less well educated people. To investigate and to analyze those phenomena, thorough research will be necessary. It could help avoid or reduce the negative impact of knowledge work and provide practical orientation and motivation for workplace innovation.

How Can Future Work Design Support the Innovative Competitiveness of Organizations as well as the Well-being and Productivity of Individuals?

To foster the opportunities and to minimize the risks of work life, the implementation of workplace innovation and advanced research should be stimulated by national and European programs. A growing number of countries are conducting or developing some kind of program aimed at labor productivity, development of competencies, learning and innovation. It is not only Germany that has a rich tradition in corresponding programs (humanization of work life, quality of work life, innovative work shaping). Examples can be found in Finland (workplace development), in Norway (value creation), the Netherlands and Belgium (social innovation), Sweden (management and work organization renewal), Ireland and the UK (workplace innovation). Europe seems at the brink of uniting the concepts of social innovation and workplace innovation. However, budgets are being cut in a number of countries, while increasing them would be more appropriate. Social innovation in organizations or workplace innovation appears to be a prerequisite for smart, sustainable and inclusive growth.

Enabling Spaces – Space Impacts Organization and Vice Versa

Thomas Fundneider and Markus Peschl

An increasingly connected and virtual world begs the question if the good old office is still essential for the success and survival of organizations. Why should knowledge workers – on a daily basis – commute to a building that quite often accommodates a social nightmare rather than the desired creative buzz? One might hear as an answer, "It is for collaboration, for communication, for creating new ideas!" However, let's be honest: Are these activities really taking place in our offices? It turns out that architecture and office design are only a small part of the problem. Rather, in many cases the organization as a whole does not provide a human- and innovation-centered working environment, because things, such as architectural, social, emotional, cognitive, organizational, epistemological, as well as technological structures are almost too complex to be thought and brought together – their integration, however, is essential for any kind of knowledge- and innovation work.

To put it simply, architecture alone is not important. It is the processes of mindfully designing an integrated and human-centered knowledge-work environment that is the focus of this paper.

Designing Human- and Innovation-Centered Work Environments

Such a design process necessarily has to cross classical disciplinary borders and integrate insights and approaches from a wide variety of sources. The authors have developed an approach (including a design process) that they refer to as *Enabling Spaces*: Consider the example of the process of knowledge creation. Here we see the necessity of integrating social, cultural, emotional, physical/architectural, as well as epistemological issues: bringing forth new knowledge is a highly fragile knowledge process, which is about intuition, listening to weak signals, deep thinking and understanding, as well as incubating vague knowledge. Due to the fragility and vulnerability of these processes it is necessary to create a kind of *container*, an Enabling Space, providing qualities such as offering an environment of protection, of enabling the free flow of knowledge, of silence, of openness for error, openness for change, as well as of collecting results in an unobtrusive manner.

These design qualities have to be translated into integrated and interdisciplinary concepts, which – in their wholeness – form an Enabling Space. Resulting from theoretical research, a scientifically sound design process has been developed over the past years, which follows several phases: (i) *Observe*: Deep and mainly qualitative observation of an organization's core processes also including its stakeholders and culture. (ii) *Core Process Model*: These research findings are reduced to a core-process model representing the essence of the organization from a knowledge and innovation perspective. (iii) *Design Patterns*: Translating these knowledge and core processes of an organization along with its culture into design qualities/patterns. (iv) *Interdisciplinary Design*: In a series of interdisciplinary workshops, these design patterns are transformed into concrete operational elements and interventions integrating the above-mentioned dimensions into an Enabling Space. (v) In a final step these concepts are realized.

One can see clearly that the creation of Enabling Spaces is a real design challenge; it has to be done for each organization individually and there are no standard solutions or simple rules. We approach this design process for working environments by deeply understanding the inner workings of an organization. It is only in a second step that architecture and design begin to translate these core organizational issues into a physical office space.

Enabling Spaces – Implications for Work Design

A project with a Corporate IT department of a globally operating engineering company provides a practical example for how an Enabling Space can be realized: Problems in service quality triggered a process of organizational re-design. We were asked to implement a future-oriented work environment including the transformation of the department's organizational culture into an innovation hub. During the Enabling Space design process, it turned out that architectural changes could not be made without closely interlocking the organizational and innovation domains. For instance, positioning the IT department as a strategic partner for the business segments required a massive training program (mainly on social skills and domain-related business understanding).

The design of work places that perform well is in most cases a result of a subtle balance of so-called polarities: *privacy*, which allows for concentration, withdrawal and solitude vs. *open office* structures where distraction, noise and skin-deep conversations are prevalent. Knowledge processes require fairly different modes of cognition: Think of reflecting, a period of intense and uninterrupted focus; then contrast this with the final phase of the roll-out of a product, where a high level of activity and collaboration by acclamation are paramount. We took this approach seriously in a project for designing a new university campus. Positioned between business, politics and culture, this rapidly growing private elite university held an architectural competition. Based on extensive research, it became clear that the space program guidelines needed a much wider interpretation. Specifically, our design (in cooperation with an architect) introduced different categories of seminar rooms, such as a standard lecture room, a project space, a dialogue room, a collaborative space and a workshop atelier in order to support exactly the core processes that make this university such a unique place.

We do not understand work environments primarily as a "place to sit" or a "place to communicate", but as a fulcrum for people's productivity and creativity. Finally, architecture has become important. But only if it is based on thoroughly understanding organizational and knowledge issues, and if these are the point of departure for the design process.

Designing Future R&D Workspaces

Sven Schimpf and Flavius Sturm

New or Old Buildings, Garages or Home Offices?

The discussion on what R&D workspaces should look like is anything but unanimous in its result. New buildings can be closely aligned to the specific requirements of the R&D department and its value network, from the overall design of the building to the building technologies and the individual workspaces. Old buildings can likewise be a trigger for innovation, as they allow individuals to adapt workspaces at relatively low cost and without much administrative overhead. Garages for example, a specific sub-set of old buildings, have become a major metaphor for the creation of successful innovations – a number of successful companies such as Hewlett Packard and Apple have used them as a first workspace. Going beyond the differentiation of R&D workspaces according to different building types, R&D employees working from home are a relatively new phenomenon with increasing potential. This option does not only create a new level of flexibility for employees, it can also reduce the number of workspaces that have to be provided by the employer.

But workspace design is not only about fostering creativity and optimizing processes and underlying cost structures. Companies such as Google or Lego use their R&D centers as a means to present their company as a hub of innovation to the outside world. The design of R&D workspaces should, to this end, not only consider R&D requirements but also the role of R&D in the overall organization and in its partner network.

Based on an analysis of current trends in R&D and requirements for workspace design, the Competence Center R&D Management at Fraunhofer IAO has described modular workspace scenarios and developed a methodology to support the process of designing future R&D workspaces. The following is a summary of key findings and contributions.

Trends in R&D

Technological advances, new collaboration models and changing requirements for R&D output are some of the major challenges facing future R&D workspaces. Aspects to be considered in the process of designing future R&D workspaces include:

- *Increased R&D networking*: What will the value network look like in the future, and who are the key partners to be involved in today's and future R&D processes?
- *Development of integrated solutions*: Which competences and process phases will be required to develop customer-oriented solutions instead of single products?
- *Higher workspace flexibility*: What should the level of flexibility for employees and for partners involved in the value network of R&D look like today and in the future?

All of these aspects call for a detailed analysis of today's and future work processes and organizational structures. The methodology developed by Fraunhofer IAO ensures that companies keep the former in mind when designing R&D workspaces.

A Methodology Supporting R&D Workspace Design

This methodology brings together the experience of two Competence Centers at Fraunhofer IAO: R&D Management and Workspace Innovation. It provides practical examples and step-by-step guidelines on how to design R&D workspaces in line with today's and future requirements. By covering all major design phases from the analysis of activity areas to the development of proven concepts and the measurement of R&D workspace performance, it allows integrating workspace profiles and requirements with the final workspace design and its performance. Throughout the design phases, modular workspace scenarios that were developed in collaboration with industrial partners are continuously mapped with profiles and requirements and adapted to the specific needs.

Scenarios for Future R&D Workspaces

R&D workspace scenarios include modules such as *creativity workshops*, *individual workspaces*, and *project rooms*. The final selection of the modules to be considered depends on the specific requirements of each single organization, or even each R&D unit. The use of modular scenarios facilitates the creation of early prototypes of the future R&D workspace based on ready-made solutions that involve the most recent developments in collaboration and communication methods and technologies and that can be easily configured and adapted to specific requirements.

Implications for Work Design

R&D and innovation are at the front-end of developing new products, services and processes. Therefore, they are key areas in which advanced work design should be applied in industrial companies. However, the intentional design of R&D workspaces is still rarely a priority within R&D departments.

Research has shown that designing physical environments can encourage processes that play a vital role in product creation, such as knowledge-sharing, learning and collaboration. It should therefore be an essential part of R&D Management to render R&D projects more effective and efficient and to benefit from the latest developments in collaboration and communication methodologies and technologies.

Work Design: Two Futures – Foxconn and the Transparent Volkswagen Factory

Frank Emspak

Our societies and workers face stark alternatives. The contrast between Foxconn in China and the Volkswagen Transparent Factory in Dresden are perhaps the greatest contrast illustrating two distinct but profitable models of work organization.

Work organization includes the level of skills needed; density and sophistication of the machinery as well as the nature of the control mechanisms, the intensity of work, and compensation. The control mechanisms range from human control over the pace and physical and mental effort, to extraneous control. Part of this spectrum is skills-biased automation where workers have a great degree of autonomy. The challenge is to develop a system that meets human needs in a sustainable fashion – given the balance of social forces confronted by working people and our society.

Important Developments in the Modern Working Environment

- The extreme mobility of capital;
- The relatively inelastic labor markets;
- The low costs of international shipping;
- The rapid international exchange of data;
- The extreme concentration of ownership/control of major corporate entities;
- The financialization of many western economies.

The extreme mobility of capital allows for investments in production in almost any area of the world; often placed in countries that combine low wages, relatively high skill levels, and the inability of the workforce to insist on improving their standard of living commensurate with the increases in productivity which the outside investments engender. Authoritarian governments are often part of this mix, guaranteeing investments and high returns-at least for a period of time.

Relatively inelastic labor markets are often linked to the extreme mobility of capital. Thus, for example, the North American Free Trade Agreement guarantees investments and free flow of capital, but prevents the equally free flow of workers. The consequence of inelastic labor markets makes it easier to impose poor working conditions and low wages as the alternatives are few. Lack of educational opportunities limits the ability of individuals to advance, thus making the labor markets even less responsive to technological change-and hence making workers even more vulnerable to their jobs being exported elsewhere.

Low costs of international shipping allow the efficient export of goods and thus, extreme capital mobility. One result is the development of worldwide supply chains. Although some recent natural disasters have called these supply chains into question, the model seems to be solidly in place. The extensive supply chains are also supported by the labor market inelasticity.

The exponentially increasing speed and density of data transfer also allows extended supply chains. While it is theoretically possible to monitor the production on each machine in a modern factory from thousands of miles away, it is very practical to monitor hourly and daily production, productivity, labor costs and also make some engineering decisions from locations remote from the actual site of production.

High levels of concentration and a belief that financial activities drive prosperity also have a significant effect on the working environment-encouraging a willingness to end many productive activities in the "advanced" industrial countries thus increasing manufacturing instability and contributing to a lack of investment infrastructure especially as it relates to the training of skilled workers-especially in the trades that are best suited for apprenticeships.

Opportunities and Risks for the Future of Working Life

- The technical capacities of production systems are such that work can be performed in a safe, energy efficient and skillful manner.
- A more equitable distribution of wealth can in fact allow for advances in all aspects of human development.
- The opposite is also true-the imposition of artificial financial structures can reduce the standard of living while maintaining a reasonable level of productivity.
- The increasing efforts at austerity rather than investment can result in the destabilization of the essential investments needed to maintain a healthy economy-as evidenced by lack of investments in training and the more obvious disintegration of some of the most prestigious private research institutions-e.g., Bell Labs.
- Short term thinking, especially as regards energy use and production pose another threat to working life.

Implications for Work Design

Work design is integral to the way in which capital is managed or controlled by the larger society. Work design is not an independent variable but subject to pressures from the environment (physical, intellectual and financial). The design of work must explicitly value human capital such as health as well as intellectual values inherent in the ability to think, design and innovate. The consequences are that while we possess the technical knowledge to design satisfying work, society (government policy) will have to confront the pressures of extreme capital mobility combined with a high level of concentration if the objectives of high productivity, high skill levels and job satisfaction are to be met.

Foxconn is an example of an extreme opposite compared to the above principles of work design. It takes a Taylorist division of labor to the limit, using thousands of low-skilled individuals to accomplish the tasks of a more mechanized, higher skilled production system. Foxconn's operations are now under pressure from their customers, who, reacting to an outcry from the end users, are demanding changes that will destabilize the low skill, low wage Foxconn model.

We see counter examples to Foxconn that use many of the positive design principles listed above in certain areas of Germany, Italy, Spain and even in the United States. But all of these examples face extreme competitive pressures and thus, in order to preserve and grow these design incubators (or successes), deliberate policies that recognize these methods of production and differences in ownership must be implemented.

Knowledge Work in the Future – What Will Remain?

Hans-Georg Schnauffer

For decades, fantastic scenarios on the future of knowledge work have been developed. Here, the perennial favorites include the paperless or the virtual office – both of these scenarios are often closely linked to various forms of speech control. Instead of typing laboriously, you just talk and you are done. But beware: not everything that appears attractive upon localized inspection of its theoretical advantages is in harmony with the overarching, if you will, 'natural laws' of knowledge work.

New Options for Knowledge Transfer versus Human Biology

So, what is it that ensures fundamental and long-term consistency in knowledge work – despite all the dynamic changes on the surface? One example is simply human biology: with regard to sensory perception of our environment via our organs, specifically eyes and ears, it is safe to assume that nothing will change. Sending and receiving knowledge will continue to take place primarily via our eyes (light) and ears (acoustics) for a long time to come. Brain research reveals that for the coming decades, futuristic fantasies – that machines will generate transferable optical or acoustic artifacts directly from individuals' thoughts – will remain just that, fantasies.

Of interest with regard to how we will work in the future is the question to what extent new technological options resulting in a shift of the sensory channels, such as from the eyes to the ears, are compatible with the biological characteristics of these organs. When looking at the various developmental avenues, e.g., those that transmit information acoustically only via speech input and output, the limits of practicability and ultimately, of perception, are quickly arrived at, especially for larger volumes of material. This is because there are essential elements that are impossible to achieve via acoustics alone, such as:

a) Getting a quick overview by means of scanning and skimming; and
b) Representing certain relationships visually using images ("a picture says more than a thousand words").

Our ears have the phenomenal ability to identify a voice, even amidst loud ambient noise, but they are not suited to "acoustic scanning." And acoustics are equally ill-suited to providing illustration. In both cases, our eyes are vastly superior to our ears and consequently, more efficient. Our eyes are much faster at generating relevance.

What Remains? Four Hypotheses!

1. *Written text and images will remain the dominant syntax of knowledge transfer!*
   In the medium term, a solution will be found for the many current disadvantages of acoustic information transfer, such as searchability. What will remain is the fundamental advantage of the eye as a sensory organ when receiving and processing large volumes of

information. A considerable amount of the roughly one gigabyte of data a person absorbs per second is, on average, absorbed by the eyes rather than the ears.
In addition, the written word has developed into a highly complex system that is taught in school over years. Therefore, this globally practiced system of conventions for representing information and knowledge has no social competition, which is why the written word will also provide the best search options for the foreseeable future.
Consequently, it is very likely that written text and images will retain their dominant role in knowledge transfer for the coming decades. What will certainly shift is the weighting between text and images. In particular, moving pictures will have distinctly more weight. The latter will, of course, also include acoustic elements, which will allow them to function independently of language and thus, globally.

2. *If the written word and images remain, paper and keyboards will, too!*
   Paper does not require electrical power and will always have the best resolution, both for text and images. Keyboards will most likely also remain the leading interface for entering writing for they are faster and quieter than speech input. Certainly, keyboards will also assume new shapes, and they will be made from different materials (such as fabric or light) so that in future they will be found in completely different environments. But this will change little with regards to the fundamental logic of generating text.
3. *If paper and keyboards remain, desks and monitors will, too!*
   Due to the advantages listed, paper will not disappear. Certainly, its volume will stagnate or decrease. But paper-free knowledge workers will probably not be the rule for a long time. Paper needs support. This means that desks and chairs will remain.
   Like keyboards, monitors will go through qualitative, material and local metamorphoses. The technical trends towards more resolution, larger surfaces, touch sensitivity, including in 3D, will continue. But it can be considered a given that knowledge workers will have such an infrastructure for decades to come. What will change is the surface or the space in which the image will be generated. It is also only a matter of time before desk surfaces and monitors will merge into one.
4. *If desks and monitors remain, walls and offices will, too.*
   Large vertical surfaces such as walls will also increasingly take on a function in respect of knowledge work. This is not only about separation, but increasingly also about support for visuals, e.g. with large screens and interactive design surfaces that will achieve a breakthrough from today's solutions, in particular for collaborative work situations. This will apply both for face-to-face processes as well as virtual ones, whose percentage will definitely increase significantly.
   Ultimately, this deductive process tells us that today's knowledge workplace – also known as the office – will fundamentally remain with us, almost certainly providing the long-term, stable constant during change that, while going through distinct developments on the surface, will still be recognizable 30 or 50 years from now.

Index of Authors

Eur Ing Dr. Keith Bevis: After twenty five years of industrial experience in manufacturing and five years as a consultant Keith Bevis joined the University of Hertfordshire to develop skills training for the automotive industry. Until 2011, he had been building sustainable business links with industry. Then Keith became the Managing Director of EValu8 -TI, leading the development of the initial infrastructure for electric vehicles across the East of England. EVs present innovation opportunities for our partners and for the University.

Prof. Dr. Kirsimarja Blomqvist is a Professor for Knowledge Management at School of Business and Vice-director for Technology Business Research Center at Lappeenranta University of Technology, Finland. She is also a regular speaker in company seminars on the topics of trust, knowledge management, innovation and collaboration. Her research has been published e.g. in California Management Review, Scandinavian Journal of Management, Creativity and Innovation Management, Research Policy, R&D Management, Technovation, and Industrial Marketing Management.

Dipl. oec. Jennifer Bredtmann is an economist and she is working at the University of Wuppertal, Interdisciplinary Center III – Management of Technical Processes as a junior researcher. She is writing her PhD on the field of networks, requirements, confidence, innovation and safety and security. She is teaching the topics of quality assurance and quality tools, and management systems. She is also an expert on the field of gender studies.

Dr.-Ing. Peter Brödner: Born in 1942, diploma of Mechanical Engineering and Dr.-Ing. from Technical University of Berlin. After 7 years as researcher at Institute of Manufacturing Automation and 13 years as project manager of large industry-driven R&D projects in the areas of flexible automation and skill-based manufacturing, he was, for the last 15 years, director of the production systems department at Institute of Work and Technology with special emphasis on computer-supported work systems and organizational change processes.

Dr. Mariana Dodourova is a senior lecturer in the University of Hertfordshire Business School. Mariana has fifteen years industrial experience prior to her involvement with academia in 2002, including six years as a manager of her own small business. Her research interests include technology and innovation management, SMEs, inter-organizational relationships and cooperation, and organizational networks. Some of her papers have appeared in European Business Review, Management Decision, Journal of Global Strategic Management and Conradi Research Review.

Stephen Downes: Senior researcher for Canada's National Research Council and a leading proponent of the use of online media and services in education. Has earned international recognition for his leading-edge work in the field of online learning (OLDaily online newsletter). Pioneered the development of learning objects and was one of the first adopters and developers of RSS content syndication in education. Downes introduced the concept of e-learning 2.0 and with George Siemens developed and defined the concept of Connectivism.

Prof. Leif Edvinsson: Key pioneering contributor to both the theory and practice of Intellectual Capital. World's first director of IC in 1991; initiated the creation of the world's first public corporate Intellectual Capital Annual Report 1994. Listed in a book by London Business Press as one of "The 50 most influential Thinkers in the World". Since 2000 Professor at Lund University on Intellectual Capital. In January 2006 appointed professor adj. at The Hong Kong Polytechnic University, later promoted to Chair Professor in 2007.

Prof. em. Frank Emspak, Ph.D.: Professor Emeritus University of Wisconsin- Extension; Director of the Center for Applied Technology (Massachusetts); Fellow- National Institute Standards and Technology; former skilled machinist and union officer. Current: Executive Producer and CEO Diversified Media Enterprises, Madison WI. www.laborradio.org; frankemspak@gmail.com

Dipl. oec. Birgit Fingerle is an innovation manager at ZBW – Leibniz Information Centre for Economics. She studied Economic & Social Sciences at the University of Lueneburg with a focus on marketing and innovation and technology management. Birgit Fingerle is responsible for ZBW's operational innovation management tasks, in particular for ZBW's open innovation activities. She is working on obtaining a professional qualification in systemic transaction analysis and depth psychology for coaching and supervision.

Stella Fleischer, M.A. studied sociology (M.A.) at the University of Münster and Sociology and Communication Science (B.A.) at the RWTH Aachen University. Currently she is a doctoral student at the Faculty of Arts and Humanities of the RWTH Aachen University and is writing her PhD thesis in sociology of work and sociology of education. Furthermore she works as a personal and scientific consultant at the Center for Learning and Knowledge Management (ZLW) of the RWTH Aachen University.

Kayano Fukuda, Ph.D. is a Visiting Scholar of National University of Singapore, and has served in the Center for Research and Development Strategy of Japan Science and Technology Agency since 2003. She received a B.A. in Agriculture from Kyoto University in 1997 and a Ph.D. in Industrial Engineering and Management from Tokyo Institute of Technology in 2008. Her current research interests are in innovation ecosystems, innovation management and science, technology and innovation policy.

Dipl.-Ing. Thomas Fundneider, MBA is one of the founders and CEO of theLivingCore (www.theLivingCore.com), specializing in the areas of innovation and strategy. He has vast experience in establishing an innovative and entrepreneurial culture and mindset in organizations. He is driven by his ambition to "get things done" and to create impact for clients.

Charlie Grantham, Ph.D. is a Viet Nam combat Veteran with 8 years in the US Army. He also had careers in academia as a Professor and in global technology companies as

Executive for Research and Development. He received his Ph.D. in Sociology from the University of Maryland in 1980 and has published seven books and several dozen technical papers. Now he is helping communities and leaders realize their potential for Sustainability by organizing a new community of practitioners. www.comm-design.net.

Uwe Hauck, M.A. studied at the University of Osnabrück and completed his master's degree in computational linguistics and artificial intelligence. He has been granted a research fellowship from IBM in Heidelberg in 1994. After that he worked as a Software engineer at Postbank AG and VR Kreditwerk AG. Since 2012 he is an advisor in the area of Online Marketing Social Media at Bausparkasse Schwäbisch Hall AG. Furthermore he is a consultant, blogger and trend researcher in the field of "Workplace of the future", Social Media and Mobile Computing.

Dr. rer. nat. Frank Hees is vice deputy head of the Institute Cluster IMA/ ZLW & IfU at RWTH Aachen University. His work focuses mainly on strategy consulting and knowledge management in companies and networks, staff and organizational development, team development and individual coaching of executives, supporting change processes, analysis and reorganization of participation and empowerment processes and training on the subjects of project and time management, creativity, systematic management, change management, network and knowledge management, qualifying people for participation, and overseeing work processes.

Dr. Gabriele Hoeborn is a civil engineer. She is working at the University of Wuppertal as a senior researcher. Her research fields are quality and sustainable development, engineering and communication, and management systems. Dr. Hoeborn teaches at the Technical University of Košice, Slovakia, and at the University of Applied Science of Zurich, Switzerland as well. She is also an expert on the field of gender studies, and has been a partner in various European projects.

Prof. Heather Hofmeister, Ph.D. is professor of Sociology, specialty Sociology of Work and co-director of the Center for Leadership and Behavior in Organizations at the Goethe-University, Frankfurt. She previously served as vice-rector for Human Resources Management and Development and professor of Sociology, specialty Gender and Life Course Research at RWTH Aachen University. Her Ph.D. is from Cornell University. Hofmeister's specialties are work and family in international comparative life course perspective and the transfer of science to practice.

Prof. Dr. Jürgen Howaldt: (1960); Social scientist; director of Sozialforschungsstelle Dortmund (Social Research Centre), a central scientific unit of TU Dortmund.

Lena Hünefeld, M.A. has studied sociology at RWTH Aachen University from 2003–2009. She has been a research assistant at the Institute of Sociology of RWTH Aachen University since April 2009. Additionally she is a member of the scientific staff of the department Sociology of Work at Goethe University in Frankfurt since September 2011.

Prof. Dr. rer. nat. Sabina Jeschke is professor at the department of mechanical engineering at the RWTH Aachen University. She is the head of the interdisciplinary Institute Cluster IMA/ ZLW & IfU. Her main research areas include complex IT-systems (e.g. cloud computing, Internet of Things, green IT & ET, semantic web services), robotics and automation (e.g. heterogeneous and cooperative robotics, cooperative agents, web services for robotics), traffic and mobility (autonomous and semi-autonomous traffic systems, international logistics, car2car & car2X models) and virtual worlds for research alliances (e.g. virtual and remote laboratories, intelligent assistants, semantic coding of specialized information).

Dipl. Soz.-Wiss. Milena Jostmeier: Social science graduate and research assistant at the Sozialforschungsstelle Dortmund, the Central Scientific Institute of the TU Dortmund, "Services and Societal Change" research unit, work areas: sociology of labor, organizational sociology, sociology of science, specialist fields: work-oriented and social innovation, knowledge production in alliances between academia and practice, employment research as a transdisciplinary field.

Dipl.-Kfm. Martin Kamprath is researcher at the Chair of Innovation Management and Entrepreneurship at the University of Potsdam. He is co-author of two books concerning the future (of work) in the creative industries. He has worked in leading media companies and in a media-based spin-off.

Dr. Anna Maria Koeck is head of the department "Innovation Management & Social Media" at ZBW. She worked at the Knowledge Management Institute at Graz University of Technology and was an associate lecturer at the Chair for Innovation and Technology Management at the University of Vienna, Austria. In her interdisciplinary dissertation she dealt with the question of how creativity in the innovation process can be supported and promoted using web applications.

Dr. Ralf Kopp: (1961); social scientist; coordinator of the research area "Learning organisation and networks" at Sozialforschungsstelle Dortmund (Social Research Centre), a central scientific unit of TU Dortmund.

Dr. Barbara Light: Barbara is an educational consultant developing and facilitating innovative professional learning programs for leaders. She is an expert in the implementation of lifelong learning systems in higher education, and worked for many years as a senior academic in a British university. She regularly speaks at conferences and holds workshops across Europe; acts as scientific adviser and evaluator to institutional European projects; and researches and writes for academic and commercial publications.

Dr. ir. Sebastiaan Meijer is associate professor Transport Systems at the Transport and Logistics division of the Royal Institute of Technology, KTH, in Stockholm, Sweden. He is building a center for gaming simulation in transport and logistics systems. Gaming simulation is used for hypothesis testing, studying behavior, knowledge and cognition, and developing new practices and procedures. Meanwhile he is part-time assistant professor at Delft University of Technology, The Netherlands. Here he leads the Railway Gaming Suite project, building gaming simulations for the Dutch railway sector.

Larissa Müller has studied political sciences and sociology at RWTH Aachen University from 2004 to 2012. She is currently a student assistant at IMA/ZLW & IfU, an institute cluster at RWTH Aachen University.

Christina Öberg, Ph.D. is an assistant professor at Lund University, Sweden. She received her Ph.D. in marketing from Linköping University. Her research interests are mergers and acquisitions, networks, customer relationships and innovation management. She has previously published in journals such as European Journal of Marketing, Journal of Business Research, International Journal of Innovation Management, Scandinavian Journal of Management, and Industrial Marketing Management.

Marc Paczian: Self-styled Mobility Junkie and elder Digital Native, is working in the IT-industry for nearly two decades. His current job at a large international Enterprise Content Management company gives him insight into many companies' working styles and how they deal with the changes in ways of working to establish the best environment for Knowledge Workers.

Prof. Dr. Markus F. Peschl is professor for cognitive science and philosophy of science at the University of Vienna. In his research he focuses on the interdisciplinary fields of innovation, cognition, and on designing spaces for knowledge creation. He has published more than 120 papers and 6 books. As a co-founder of theLivingCore he is head of the scientific advisory board. See also: http://www.univie.ac.at/knowledge/peschl/

Prof. Frank Pot, Ph.D.: (1945); social scientist: professor of social innovation of work and employment, Radboud University Nijmegen.

Celina Proch, M.A. holds a position as research assistant at the chair of sociology of work at the Goethe University, Frankfurt. She began her training in business management and advertising and spent several years working in public relations. Proch continued her advanced education at RWTH Aachen University where she majored in sociology, psychology and political science before continuing with her doctoral work, first in Aachen, then in Frankfurt.

Assoc. Prof. Lauge Baungaard Rasmussen is a sociologist, employed at the Department of Management Engineering at The Technical University of Denmark as associate professor. He has written books and articles about how to facilitate change in organizations, communities and networks. He is in particular focused on how qualitative and quantitative methods can interact, sustaining creativity, strategy development and innovative policy decisions in organizations, communities and networks.

Dr. Anja Richert is managing director of the Center for Learning and Knowledge Management (ZLW) of the RWTH Aachen University. Her main areas of research are the development of agile turbulence-tolerant processes and organizational concepts for knowledge and technology-intensive organizations, the development of knowledge management solutions and e-learning tools (e.g. knowledge maps) for various fields, as well as accompanying research for complex organizational development processes in heterogeneous research networks.

Yvonne Salazar, M.A.: Human resources development and adult education. She has focused in her professional career on improving learning transfer and learning efficiency as well as skills management. Important professional functions: advisor to the Argentinean government on the reform of the vocational education system, head of staff development at the Berlin Municipal Sanitation Service, CEO of a training and consulting agency. Today: project manager of Global Training Business Development at Festo Didactic, Denkendorf, Germany.

Dr. Sven Schimpf works in the Competence Center R&D Management at the Fraunhofer Institute for Industrial Engineering IAO. Throughout his career, he has been involved in various consulting projects supporting industrial R&D in different disciplines from the set-up of idea management systems and methods for long-term planning to the implementation of process structures including the identification and evaluation of suitable technologies.

Dipl.-Kfm. Hans-Georg Schnauffer has been a specialist at ThyssenKrupp AG in the corporate center Corporate Development responsible for strategic knowledge management. Previous to this he managed various consultancy and research projects for knowledge and innovation management at the Fraunhofer-Gesellschaft. Specialisms: knowledge networks, innovation processes, trend identification and organizational learning. Member of the advisory board of the Federal Ministry of Economics and Technology's initiative "Ready for the Knowledge Competition".

Prof. Dr. rer. oec., Dipl.-Kfm. Markus G. Schwering: Born in 1971, is a Professor of Business Economics at the University of Applied Sciences in Münster and Research Professor at the Institute for Applied Innovation Research at the Ruhr-University in Bochum.

Agata Siuda, M.A. works as a scientific assistant in the interdisciplinary research project City2020+ at the Human Technology Centre (HumTec) at the RWTH Aachen University. She studied geography, economic geography and urban planning and transport at the RWTH and graduated in March 2009. At the moment she is doing her PH.D. within the field of cultural geography.

Prof. Dr. phil., Dipl.-Soz.-Wiss. Frank Striewe: Born in 1969, is a Professor of Business Economics at the University of Applied Sciences in Münster and Research Professor at the Institute for Applied Innovation Research at the Ruhr-University in Bochum.

Dipl. oec. Flavius Sturm works in the Competence Center R&D Management at the Fraunhofer Institute for Industrial Engineering IAO. After having received a Master degree in Economics from the University of Hannover in 2002, Flavius Sturm joined the R&D Management Competence Center at Fraunhofer IAO, where he gained extensive experience in technology and innovation management projects. He currently heads the Center for Corporate Development at Fraunhofer IAO and is project manager of "R&D Workspace 2015+".

Prof. Dr. Klaus Tochtermann has been the director of ZBW since 2010 and is a Professor of Computer Science at the Chair for Media Informatics at Kiel University (Germany). He was Professor at Graz University of Technology and the director of Know-Center, Austria's first industry-based research institute on knowledge management. His research interests include linked open data, semantic technologies, open innovation and future internet.

Patrizio Tonelli, Ph.D. is PhD of history and politics. At the University of Bologna (Italy) studied the post 1945 Italian and international trade union movement. Actually is researcher in "Work tendencies" area of Fundación SOL, coordinating training programs for union leaders and studying working conditions developments. He coordinates also research projects at Centre for Industrial Relations at the Economic Science Faculty (FACEA) of Universidad Central.

Sven Trantow, M.A. is leader of the "Innovation Research and Futurology" research group and the "International Monitoring" project at the Institute Cluster IMA/ ZLW & IfU – RWTH Aachen University. His research focuses on the future development of economy and work, the formation of innovations, on the characteristics of innovative systems, and on concepts of organizational change and monitoring.

Eilif Trondsen, Ph.D. is the Director at Strategic Business Insights (SBI) in Menlo Park, California where he has led Virtual Worlds @ Work for four years. The focus area of Dr. Trondsen's research and consulting at SBI – a spin-out of SRI International (formerly Stanford Research Institute) – is the use of technology for innovation, learning and performance improvement. He has over 32 years' experience at SBI and at SRI International, leading or contributing to a variety of projects for U.S. and foreign clients in the private and public sectors.

FH-Prof. Mag. Dr. Thomas Wallner holds a Professorship for System Theory and Supply Chain Management at the University of Applied Sciences in Steyr, Austria. His experience includes 20 years of Business Consultancy and Management Training. He is currently project manager and co-leading scientist in a major research project on the application of High Performance Work Systems. Holding a J.D., he studied Physics, Communication Science, Political Science and Law in Vienna and General Management in New York City.

Dr. Werner Wobbe works at the European Commission's Research and Innovation Department supporting advisory committees like High Level Group of economist "Innovation for Growth" or that of "Knowledge Economists". He was acting Head of the Unit "Science and Technology Foresight" and head of sector "Industrial Structures" in the enterprise and industry department. He is an author and editor of several books and reports on new manufacturing systems, work, social and economic developments, and foresight.